T0149001

J. R. R. TOLKIEN

INSPIRING LIVES

J. R. R. TOLKIEN

INSPIRING LIVES

ROBERT S. BLACKHAM

First published 2012
This edition published 2019

The History Press
97 St. George's Place, Cheltenham, Gloucestershire, GL50 3QB
www.thehistorypress.co.uk

British Library Cataloguing in Publication Data.
A catalogue record for this book is available from the British Library.

ISBN 978 0 7509 9227 5

Typesetting and origination by The History Press
Printed and bound in Great Britain by TJ International Ltd.

MIX
Paper from
responsible sources
FSC® C013056

• CONTENTS •

• INTRODUCTION •

WITH THE MAKING OF six blockbuster movies in the late twentieth and early twenty-first century based on J.R.R. Tolkien's most famous books, *The Lord of the Rings* and *The Hobbit*, Tolkien has reached an even greater audience than ever before; although he had already reached many millions of readers during his lifetime and after his death in 1973.

Born in southern Africa to English parents, Arthur and Mabel Tolkien, Tolkien travelled to England at the age of 3. His childhood, in and around the Birmingham area, was filled with love but also tragedy as he was an orphan by the age of 12.

King Edward's School and religion, the Roman Catholic faith, became the bedrock of his teenage years in Birmingham and he was to meet his future wife, Edith Bratt, also an orphan, when he was aged 16. But the course of true love for the couple had many pitfalls as they were forcibly separated till Tolkien reached the age of 21.

Tolkien went and studied at Exeter College, Oxford between 1911 and 1915, and after achieving a first-class honours degree he was swept up by world events, joining the British Army and fighting in the First World War in the Battle of the Somme in France in 1916. Also that year he married Edith Bratt.

Tolkien's military career was cut short by illness but during this time he started writing and creating his fictional world of Middle-earth, which was to be a lifelong project. After the war he returned to Oxford and then for a time was at the University of Leeds, returning to Oxford as a professor in 1925.

Tolkien lived in Oxford for most of the rest of his life and here his life followed many paths, as a father and family man to four children, as dedicated lecturer and tutor to his students, as an active member of Oxford literary groups like the Inklings, and as a writer. Tolkien not only wrote his great fantasy works but also poetry, literary criticism, philology and translation.

By the 1960s Tolkien's fame was global due mostly to *The Hobbit* and *The Lord of the Rings*, but fame came at a cost as his private life was often plagued by over-enthusiastic 'fans' and this eventually drove him and Edith to leave Oxford.

This miscellany is designed to give new and old Tolkien fans, whether they have come to Tolkien though his books or the films, an insight into one of the great writers of the twentieth century. Many years after his death new generations are discovering his works and, with the global availability of the films of his books, most of the population of the world in the twenty-first century will know the name Tolkien.

• THE TOLKIEN SOCIETY •

J.R.R. Tolkien,
Merton College,
1958. (Courtesy
of Andy Compton.
ADC Books)

THE TOLKIEN SOCIETY (FOUNDED by Vera Chapman
in 1969 to further interest in the life and works of
J.R.R. Tolkien, CBE, the author of *The Hobbit*, *The
Lord of the Rings* and other works of fiction and phil-
ological study) is proud to have Robert Blackham

as a member and a work such as this adding to the scholarship on our favourite author.

Based in the United Kingdom and registered as an independent, non-profit making charity, the society boasts an international membership in over forty countries. The society helps to bring together those with like minds, both formally and informally, with gatherings locally or nationally throughout the year. Recently we have been involved in weekend events in May based at Sarehole Mill and the setting up of the Shire Country Park, and we are continuing to work with other groups in the area on other Tolkien-related projects.

Our three main events at a national level are: the Annual General Meeting and Dinner, held in the spring in a different town or city in the UK each year; the Seminar, which takes place in the summer and presents a programme of talks on a Tolkien-related subject; and Oxonmoot, held over a weekend in September in an Oxford college, with a range of activities such as talks, discussions, slideshows and a costume party.

The society produces two publications: the bulletin, *Amon Hen*, appears six times a year, with Tolkien-related reviews, news, letters, artwork and articles, both humorous and serious; the annual journal, *Mallorn*, is more serious in nature, with longer critical articles, reviews and essays.

Within the society there are local groups spread throughout Britain and the world called 'Smials' (after hobbit homes). Here both members and non-members can gather to discuss Tolkien's works, as well as other writers and topics. The formality and seriousness of meetings varies depending on the members. In addition to these there are Special Interest Groups that cover topics such as collecting, biography and Tolkien's languages. For young members there is the active group 'Entings', which has its own section in the society bulletin.

The society has a website that provides members and non-members with general information about itself and the world of Tolkien: http://www.tolkien-society.org.

The Tolkien Society, 2012
Hon. Pres.: the late Professor J.R.R. Tolkien, CBE

in perpetuo
Hon. Vice Pres. Priscilla Tolkien
Founded in 1969 by Vera Chapman

Registered Charity No. 273809

• TIMELINE •

1892 3 January	John Ronald Reuel Tolkien (known as Ronald) born in Bloemfontein, Orange Free State, southern Africa, to Arthur and Mabel Tolkien.
1894 17 February	Hilary Arthur Reuel Tolkien born.
1895 spring	Mabel and the Tolkien brothers come to England.
1896 15 February	Arthur Tolkien dies after suffering a severe haemorrhage.
1896 summer	Mabel and the Tolkien brothers move to the small hamlet of Sarehole on the edge of Birmingham.
1900	Mabel and the Tolkien brothers move to Moseley Village in Birmingham.
1901	Mabel and the Tolkien brothers move to King's Heath in Birmingham.

1902	Mabel and the Tolkien brothers move to Oliver Road in Edgbaston, Birmingham.
1904 14 November	Mabel dies from diabetes at the age of 34.
1905	The Tolkien brothers move to Stirling Road in Edgbaston to live with their Aunt Beatrice.
1908	The Tolkien brothers move to Duchess Road, Edgbaston and Ronald meets Edith Bratt, his future wife.
1910	The Tolkien brothers move to Highfield Road, Edgbaston.
1911 October	Ronald goes to Exeter College, Oxford.
1913 8 January	Ronald is reunited with Edith Bratt in Cheltenham.
1915 summer	Ronald takes his final examinations and is awarded a first-class honours degree and then enters military service in the 13th Lancashire Fusiliers.
1916 22 March	Ronald marries Edith Bratt at St Mary Immaculate church in Warwick.
1916 4 June	Ronald embarks for France and takes part in the Battle of the Somme between July and October.
1916 November	Ronald returns to England with trench fever and does not go overseas again during the First World War.

1918 **November**	*Ronald and Edith move to Oxford with their first son, John, and Ronald starts to work for the* New English Dictionary.
1920 **October**	*Ronald moves to the University of Leeds as reader in English Language and his second son, Michael, is born; his family join him in 1921.*
1925 **summer**	*Ronald is elected Rawlinson and Bosworth professor of Anglo-Saxon in Oxford and buys 22 Northmoor Road in north Oxford.*
1929	*Ronald and Edith's daughter, Priscilla, is born.*
1930	*The Tolkien family move to 20 Northmoor Road.*
1937	*In the autumn* The Hobbit *is published and Ronald starts to write* The Lord of the Rings.
1945 **autumn**	*Ronald becomes Merton Professor of English and Literature and a fellow of Merton College Oxford.*
1947	*The Tolkiens move to Manor Road, Oxford.*
1949	The Lord of the Rings *is completed.*
1950	*The Tolkiens move to Holywell Street, Oxford.*
1953	*Ronald and Edith move to Sandfield Road in Oxford.*

1954	*The first two volumes of* The Lord of the Rings *are published.*
1955	*The third volume of* The Lord of the Rings *is published.*
1959	*Ronald retires from Merton College.*
1968	*Ronald and Edith leave Oxford to live in Lakeside Road, Poole.*
1971	*Edith dies aged 82.*
1972	*Ronald moves back to Oxford and lives in rooms on Merton Street.*
1973	*Ronald dies aged 81.*

1

TOLKIEN AND THE SILVER SCREEN

THE STORY OF TOLKIEN'S works making it from the printed word to the film screen has as many twists and turns as the plots of his books, and the actual sums of money paid for the film rights may well be lost in the mists of time, in a far-off land, a long long time ago ...

In 1964 William L. Snyder obtained the rights to *The Hobbit* and other works by Tolkien; these rights were to last until 30 June 1966 and the sum of money paid was always said to have been peanuts. Snyder got Gene Deitch, the animator behind

Tom and Jerry, to work on making a feature-length animated movie of *The Hobbit*, and Deitch worked with Bill Bernal on the screenplay for the movie. It is said that the screenplay was loosely based on the book but that a female character was created in the form of a princess in order to tone down Bilbo Baggins' bachelor status!

In early 1966 Deitch went to New York with a much-changed script for *The Hobbit*, having by this time read *The Lord of the Rings*. This was to be presented to 20th Century Fox, but Snyder asked for too much money and the deal fell through. But Snyder could see that there was money to be made from the film rights as by this time the Tolkien phenomenon had taken off. He got Deitch to make a 12-minute animated movie of *The Hobbit*; this was done in Prague and took thirty days to make, with the brilliant Czech illustrator Adolf Born working on the visual effects.

The film arrived in New York on 29 June 1966. Snyder had booked a small projector room in Manhattan and the 12-minute animated film of *The Hobbit* was shown on 30 June. Deitch literally went and got people off the street to come and see the film, giving them a dime, which they handed

back to him to pay to see the film. After the showing, members of the audience were asked to sign
a paper to say that they had paid to see the full-
colour animated film of *The Hobbit* on 30 June 1966.
Because of this, Snyder retained the film rights to all
of Tolkien's work and sold them back to Tolkien for
around $100,000, a very large sum of money at the
time. The 12-minute 35mm print of the film was
rediscovered in January 2012 and can be seen on
the internet (Google 'Deitch Hobbit').

Elven armour from *The Lord of the Rings* film trilogy. (Vëon
Menelion/PKM at the Wikimedia Project/Wikimedia Commons)

Tolkien's Aunt Grace, his father Arthur's younger sister, told Tolkien tales of the Tolkien family roots in Europe and how one relation, George von Hohenzollern, had fought with Archduke Ferdinand at the Siege of Vienna in 1529. George had raided the Turkish lines and captured the sultan's standard and had been give the nickname **Tollkubn,** *which meant 'foolhardy', and this nickname persisted. The family had moved to France but in 1794 had fled to England to escape the French Revolution and had started to use the surname Tolkien.*

The Tolkiens had blended into English life by the nineteenth century and had become clock, watch and piano makers. Piano making had been Tolkien's grandfather John Benjamin Tolkien's business in Birmingham but the business had become bankrupt in 1877.

There are tales that during the Beatles' flower-power period they looked into making a film of *The Lord of the Rings* in which Paul McCartney was to play Frodo with John Lennon as Gollum, George Harrison as Gandalf, and Ringo Starr as Sam, however this did not make it to the silver screen.

Tolkien again sold the film rights to *The Hobbit* and *The Lord of the Rings* in 1969 to United Artists, reputedly for $250,000 although some sources give a much lower sum of money. The money is believed to have been used to pay off a tax bill. Tolkien, and after his death the Tolkien Estate, retained a 7.5 per cent royalty for any future films made from the two books. United Artists employed John Boorman to produce a screenplay for *The Lord of the Rings* in 1970 but this never went into production.

A Gollum sculpture at the Wax Museum, Mexico City. (Vic201401/ Wikimedia Commons)

In 1976 United Artists sold the film rights to Tolkien's works to the Saul Zaentz Company. They, through a company called Middle-earth Enterprises, produced an animated film called *The Lord of the Rings*, which was released in 1978. The film was directed by Ralph Bakshi and is based on the first half of *The Lord of the Rings*; the film is made up of live footage and animation. The live footage is rotoscoped – a method where live images are traced on to cels (celluloid transparent sheets) to convert them into animations – giving the film a consistent look. The film received mixed reviews from the critics but was a financial success and in later years influenced Peter Jackson in the making of his *The Lord of the Rings* films.

But before this, an animated film entitled *The Hobbit* was released in 1977, produced by Rankin/ Bass and directed by Arthur Rankin Jr and Jules Bass. The film ran for 78 minutes and could be said to have been the prequel to *The Lord of the Rings*. They released an animated movie of the third book of the trilogy, *The Return of the King*, in 1979; this film ran for 97 minutes, so was a much-compressed version of the book, but held the basic storyline together.

The Hobbit *was not what you would call a planned book by Tolkien, but started one day when he was marking examination papers. A student had left a blank page and Tolkien wrote on the page 'In a hole in the ground there lived a Hobbit' (H. Carpenter, 'The Storyteller',* **J.R.R. Tolkien: a Biography***). Tolkien did not know what a Hobbit was but started writing the story in 1930/1931 and by 1932 he was able to show his friend C.S. Lewis an almost completed manuscript.*

The Lord of the Rings twenty-first-century film trilogy was directed by Peter Jackson; the three-film project took eight years to make and cost $285 million. The films were made in New Zealand and distributed by New Line Cinema. The films take their titles from the three books that make up *The Lord of the Rings*, being *The Fellowship of the Ring* (2001), *The Two Towers* (2002) and *The Return of the King* (2003). The films follow Tolkien's basic plot but flow through the storyline in a form that is easy to follow for the filmgoer, although they do leave out some of the plot and some of the characters, notably Tom Bombadil.

In 2002 a 2,000-page yellowing handwritten manuscript written by Tolkien, translating and appraising the epic poem **Beowulf,** *was found in the Bodleian Library.* **Beowulf** *became a movie in 2007 and could be viewed in 3D as well as 2D at cinemas worldwide.*

The epic tale, set in Tolkien's fictional world of Middle-earth, is based around the destruction of the One Ring, made and owned by the Dark Lord Sauron. At the start of the first film, the One Ring is in the hands of Bilbo Baggins and is then given to his adopted heir Frodo Baggins, both Hobbits. Frodo is accompanied by the Fellowship of the Ring, made up of the Hobbits Sam, Merry and Pippin; Gandalf the Wizard, Gimli the Dwarf, Legolas the Elf, Boromir the Man from Gondor, and Strider the Ranger. The fellowship is on a quest to destroy the One Ring in the Cracks of Doom, but by the end of the first film the fellowship is broken up.

The next two films follow the adventures of the various surviving members of the fellowship and the other characters, both good and bad – notably the treacherous Gollum, himself once an 'owner' of the One Ring. The final film reaches a climax with

The Lord of the Rings fantasy armour from the Texas Renaissance Festival, 2008. (Jeremy Van Dyke/Magnus Manske/ Wikimedia Commons)

Visiting the Hobbits, Matamata. (Tara Hunt/Vëon Menelion/
Wikimedia Commons)

the destruction of the One Ring and the return of the Hobbits to a much-changed homeland, the Shire. The three films have grossed just under $3 billion worldwide to date.

Following the success of the three films based on the *The Lord of the Rings*, three further films, based on *The Hobbit* are being produced. They are *The Hobbit: An Unexpected Journey* (2012), *The Hobbit: The Desolation of Smaug* (2013), *The Hobbit: There and Back Again* (2014).

Tolkien started writing **The Lord of the Rings** *in 1937 and finished it in 1949, a total of twelve years in all. It was first published in three volumes,* **The Fellowship of the Ring** *and* **The Two Towers** *in 1954, and* **The Return of the King** *in 1956. It was published in three volumes because the publisher, George Allen & Unwin Ltd, were concerned that if it was sold as one book it would make a loss and so the three-book trilogy was born into the literary world.*

Tolkien told Paul Drayton and Humphrey Carpenter, who later became his biographer, that he thought of himself as a Hobbit and identified himself with the Hobbit called Hugo Bracegirdle who is a guest at Bilbo's farewell party at the start of **The Lord of the Rings.** *Hugo is notable for borrowing books and failing to return them.*

2

SOUTHERN AFRICA

JOHN RONALD REUEL TOLKIEN was born on 3 January 1892 in Bloemfontein in the Orange Free State in southern Africa, but for most of his life he preferred to be called by his second Christian name, Ronald. He was baptised in St Andrew and St Michael Anglican Cathedral on 31 January 1892. His parents, Arthur and Mabel Tolkien, had married in Cape Town in 1891 and honeymooned at Sea Point, located between Signal Hill and the Atlantic Ocean, a short distance west of Cape Town's city centre.

Arthur and Mabel originally met in what today are the southern suburbs of the city of Birmingham in England. They had become engaged three years earlier, but Mabel's father would not let her marry Arthur until she was 21. Arthur had moved to southern Africa a year before, leaving his position at Lloyds Bank in Birmingham to seek a better life there. Mabel joined Arthur in southern Africa in 1891.

After working in a number of branches of Bank of Africa, Arthur Tolkien was appointed manager of the bank's branch on Maitland Street in Bloemfontein in 1890. The newly married couple lived in Bank House, next door to the bank, with a large garden behind the house; the house is now long gone, washed away by a flood in the 1920s. Mabel was devoted to Arthur and although they did not know it at the time, Bank House was to be their only family home together.

Mabel's new life was far removed from her life as a single woman back in Birmingham; she had a staff of servants, both black, coloured and white immigrants, and she appears to have treated them equally, most likely due to her Nonconformist background in Birmingham. This equal treatment was unusual for the time.

Life for Mabel in Bloemfontein had its ups and downs. Some of the time she would accompany Arthur to dinner parties and other social events and other times she would be alone, as Arthur was busy with bank business or learning Dutch, the

Maitland Street, Bloemfontein in the 1980s.

One of Tolkien's childhood memories of his time at Sarehole was to reemerge later when writing **The Lord of the Rings;** *Hilary Tolkien recalled in later life that his brother was once chased by a local farmer for picking mushrooms on his land. The Tolkien brothers nicknamed the farmer the 'Black Ogre'. In* **The Lord of the Rings,** *Frodo, as a young Hobbit, is caught picking mushrooms on Farmer Maggot's land. Tolkien uses the term 'maggot' as a term of abuse when the Orcs, the Dark Lord's soldiers, are arguing with one another in* **The Lord of the Rings.** *So, could calling the farmer Maggot be a joke or Tolkien's way of getting revenge on the farmer who chased him as a young boy?*

language of trade and government in the Orange Free State. They played golf together but Mabel only had second-hand clubs and tended to lose golf balls, so Arthur cut back on her housekeeping allowance to redress the loss of the balls. She reputedly cut back on his favourite foods until he finally relented and reinstated her full housekeeping allowance.

Tolkien and his brother Hilary would sometimes play with the Oratory kitchen cat after they had eaten their breakfast in the refectory, by putting it into a rotary food hatch and spinning it around. The cat, apparently, didn't seem to mind.

The Birmingham Oratory have a number of 'relics', held in a private collection, from Tolkien's time living in Edgbaston; these include Father Francis's executor's account book, share certificates from Arthur Tolkien's investment in southern Africa and Mabel Tolkien's travel trunk, used when she came to Birmingham for a 'holiday' in 1895. She was never to return to southern Africa due to Arthur's death in 1896.

The climate in Bloemfontein was not to Mabel's liking: it was too hot in the summer and too cold and dry in the winter. Basically, she thought it was a horrible place.

Ronald's brother Hilary was born on 17 February 1894.

In the summer, the Tolkien brothers would not be allowed out in the garden from mid morning until late afternoon to keep them out of the hot African sun.

Adventures started for Tolkien at a very early age: a black servant called Isaak took the baby Tolkien home to his kraal to show the people there, with some pleasure, what a white baby looked like. This caused great distress at Bank House, but Isaak was not sacked from his job and when his own son was born he named him Isaak Mister Tolkien Victor (the Victor part of the name in honour of Queen Victoria).

Wildlife was all around Bloemfontein, which had only been founded some forty-five years previously; there were lions, wolves, wild dogs and jackals on the veldt outside the town, but the garden of Bank House had its own share of wild creatures. There were snakes in the woodshed and rain spiders (or huntsman spiders) lurking in the long grass: as the name implies, they hunt just before or just after a rainstorm. They can grow to the size of a dinner plate and were locally called tarantulas. When Tolkien had just started to take his first steps in the garden on a summer day he was bitten by a rain spider; his nurse came to the rescue and sucked the venom from the bite. Rain spiders do not hunt using a web but grab their prey, unlike the large evil spiders that were to appear in his fictional world of Middle-earth in the form of Shelob in *The Lord of the Rings,* and the spiders that live in Mirkwood in *The Hobbit*.

SS *Guelph.*

Tolkien was not coping with the hot summer weather and his health was a constant worry to Mabel, so she decided to take him and his brother back to England and hoped that Arthur would follow them later when on leave from the bank. So in the spring of 1895 Mabel and her two sons took the 700-mile train journey from Bloemfontein to Cape Town and then on the SS *Guelph* for the three-week sea voyage back to England. Arthur hired a nurse to help Mabel look after her sons on the voyage.

One of the positions Tolkien held at Merton College was as a member of the College Wine Committee and for a time he was Steward of Common Room. In this role, he held the master key to the college cellar, which he once took on holiday with him, putting the college into a bit of a spin.

3

PIPE SMOKING IN FICTION AND LIFE

TOLKIEN WAS A KEEN pipe smoker for most of his adult life; in later years he did claim that he possibly owed his own addiction to this habit to seeing Father Francis Morgan smoking a cherrywood pipe at Oratory House in Rednal. This was the only place that Tolkien ever saw Father Francis smoking but back then the public image of priests was vigorously controlled by the Church: they were not allowed to smoke in public and also not allowed to go to the theatre.

By the time Tolkien was at Exeter College he was a committed smoker, mostly smoking a pipe but sometimes cigarettes. Smoking was socially acceptable back then and a lot cheaper than it is today, and Tolkien was most happy when with his fellow students talking and smoking late into the evening.

Tolkien once wrote: 'Every morning I wake up and think, good another 24 hours' pipe-smoking' (John Ezard, the *Guardian*, 1991). His tobacco of choice appears to have been Capstan Medium Navy Cut and apparently his family kept all their nuts and bolts and other small items in this brand of tobacco tin.

The science fiction writer John Wyndham, most famous for the book **The Day of the Triffids,** *lived in Edgbaston at the same time as Tolkien, he was nine years younger than Tolkien but was also a Roman Catholic so most likely attended The Oratory Church. He left Edgbaston in 1911 when his parents separated, which was also the same time Tolkien went to Oxford.*

Tolkien's interest in languages started at an early age when his mother, Mabel, started to teach him Latin and he began creating his own languages. His mother's sister Edith Incledon (her married name) lived in Barnt Green just outside Birmingham and had two daughters, Mary and Marjorie. They also invented their own language called 'Animalic' and this was made mostly from animal names where, for example, **Dog** *meant* **You.** *One could say that the gift of language ran in the family.*

The tobacco of Middle-earth is pipe-weed, also called Halflings' leaf or just leaf. It originally came from Númenor but also grew well in the southern part of Midde-earth. It could be grown in the north of Gondor in places like Longbottom and Bree but only with great care. Hobbits in Bree appear to have been the first to develop the art of smoking, and this is where a strain of tobacco called Southlinch was grown. The Prancing Pony inn became a centre for pipe smoking, and it was here that travellers such as Dwarves, Rangers and Wizards like Gandalf were first introduced to the habit of smoking. There are many different strains of pipe-weed in Middle-earth; some of the most famous are from the Southfarthing and include Longbottom Leaf, considered to be finest variety, Old Toby and Southern Star.

Pipe smoking is mentioned frequently in *The Hobbit* and *The Lord of the Rings*. The Hobbits were renowned pipe smokers and Gandalf, Aragorn and Gimli also enjoyed the habit, although Legolas disapproved as did all Elves.

London had its own bit of Middle-earth during the 1960s: there was a club called Middle-earth where the late great John Peel sometimes played the records and also a market in Kensington called Gandalf's Garden.

4

BIRMINGHAM DAYS

IN THE SPRING OF 1895, Tolkien, his brother Hilary and mother Mabel arrived at Southampton and were met by Mabel's younger sister Jane, who was to play a major role in the brothers' later life. They all travelled by train from Southampton to, most likely, Birmingham New Street Station, a place that was very familiar to Jane as she had used the station on her journeys to and from school and had even passed letters from her sister Mabel to Arthur Tolkien there.

From New Street Station they would have taken the steam tram along the Moseley Road, through Moseley Village then up the hill on Alcester Road to King's Heath. They then had a short walk to Ashfield Road to Mabel's parents' new home at 9 Ashfield

The Hobbit *has sold over 100 million copies to date but was originally written as a story that Tolkien read to his children on dark winter evenings, although by 1936 his three sons had outgrown bedtime stories. Elaine Griffiths, a family friend, was shown the typed copy of* **The Hobbit** *and was so impressed with it that she got Susan Dagnall, who worked at George Allen and Unwin, the publishers, to read it – they subsequently published it in on 21 September 1937.*

Stanley Unwin made one final marketing check on **The Hobbit** *before publishing it: he got his son Rayner, who was 10 years old at the time, to read it, reasoning that children were the best judges of children's books. Rayner gave* **The Hobbit** *a favourable report and stated that it was suitable for children aged 5–9 years old, just a little younger than he was at the time. He was paid 1s for his efforts and report. The book's first print run of 1,500 copies sold out in two months.*

The Hobbit *was reprinted in 1946. Tolkien had revised it while they were living at Manor Road, Oxford, to enable the One Ring and Gollum to fit better into his new book* **The Lord of the Rings.** **Farmer Giles of Ham** *was also published in 1946.*

Road. While Mabel had been in Bloemfontein her parents had moved from their home in Trafalgar Road, Moseley, to King's Heath.

Spring moved on into summer and Tolkien's health improved in the English climate. Tolkien's father Arthur was missing his family but business at the bank kept preventing him from coming to England to join them. Bad news reached Ashfield Road in the November of that year, however: Arthur had suffered an attack of rheumatic fever and, although he was over the worst of the illness, he was not well enough to make the long journey to England to join his family.

Christmas was a worrying time for Mabel with Arthur still unwell in Bloemfontein, but for the Tolkien brothers it was a time of excitement and presents as this was their first English Christmas. By January, Mabel was making plans to return to Bloemfontein to look after Arthur who was still unwell. In mid-February Tolkien got his nurse to write a letter to his father to tell him they were returning home and that he may not recognise him and his brother Hilary as they had grown so much during their time in England. Sadly the letter was never sent, as a telegram arrived at Ashfield Road to tell Mabel that Arthur had suffered a haemorrhage and had died the next day, on 15 February 1896. He was buried in Bloemfontein.

There was now nothing for Mabel and the boys in Bloemfontein as the house with the bank would have gone to its new manager. Some of Arthur's personal effects must have been returned to Mabel, but basically all she possessed was what she had brought with her for a holiday. Her only money came from some shares in the Bonanza Mines that Arthur had purchased while at the bank, which would provide a modest income of 30*s* a week.

When Mabel was living in Bloemfontein she was head of a busy household, but now she found herself a single parent with two sons, and living with her parents. It was very crowded, as also in the house on Ashfield Road were her brother William and her sister Jane. To top it all, there was also a lodger at Ashfield Road, a young man called Edwin Neave, an insurance clerk, who would serenade Jane on his banjo. Young Tolkien was very taken by the banjo playing and wished to have a banjo of his own. Neave became engaged to Jane and they were married much later in Manchester in 1905.

Mabel needed to set up home on her own to escape her extended Suffield family in the crowded house in Ashfield Road. She did not want to be too far away from her family, so in the summer of 1896 she rented a cottage; we would call it a semi-detached house, on Wake Green Road in the nearby hamlet of Sarehole.

John Suffield, Tolkien's grandfather, had a Jeyes Fluid franchise in Birmingham. At the time, Jeyes Fluid was a relatively new product on the market. It was mainly used as an outdoor disinfectant but had also been used in bathwater as a cure for scarlet fever.

John Suffield lived to the ripe old age of 97 and was a skilled draughtsman who could write 'the Lord's Prayer' in copperplate inside a circle drawn around a sixpence; his drawing skills and even his style of drawing appear to have been inherited by Tolkien.

Back then the house was known as 5 Gracewell Cottages and was only a few years old when Mabel and the Tolkien brothers rented it. It had originally been built for the servants and retainers of the wealthy local solicitor A.H. Foster, who owned much of the land and property around the hamlet of Sarehole, including Sarehole Mill.

The hamlet of Sarehole was outside Birmingham in the county of Worcestershire at the time the Tolkien family lived there, and was around 2 miles from Mabel's parents' home in King's Heath.

This was a golden time in Ronald Tolkien's life, and he was taught by his mother and, later, by his Aunt Jane who was a teacher at King Edward's Bath Row School. While teaching she had taken a science degree at Mason College in Birmingham city centre. This was a very unusual thing for a woman to have undertaken at the time and shows what an independent and modern lady Tolkien's Aunt Jane was.

In 1957 Tolkien was given the International Fantasy Award, a large cigarette lighter shaped like a space rocket, not much use to a pipe smoker it must be said!

When Tolkien was not studying there were wonderful places to see and explore in the Worcestershire countryside around the hamlet. He once wrote:

> Though a Tolkien by name, I am a Suffield by tastes, talent and upbringing.

Of Worcestershire, he said:

> Any corner of that county (however fair or squalid) is in an indefinable way 'home' to me, as no other part of the world is.
>
> (Carpenter, H., *J. R. R. Tolkien: a Biography*)

In a rare interview in 1966, reproduced by John Ezard in the *Guardian* in 1991, Tolkien described how important the little hamlet of Sarehole on the rural edge of Birmingham had been in the development of his fictional vision:

> It was a kind of lost paradise ... There was an old mill that really did grind corn with two millers, a great big pond with swans on it, a sandpit, a

wonderful dell with flowers, a few old-fashioned village houses and, further away, a stream with another mill ...

Further on in the article he re-emphasises the importance of his childhood memories of the area:

I could draw you a map of every inch of it. I loved it with an (intense) love ... I was brought up in considerable poverty, but I was happy running about in that country. I took the idea of the hobbits from the village people and children ...

When Tolkien and his brother Hilary were living at Duchess Road, Edith, who later became Tolkien's wife, would get Annie, the housemaid, to smuggle food from the kitchen when their landlady Mrs Faulkner was out. They would then have clandestine feasts in Edith's bedroom, which was something Edith had done while being a boarder at Dresden House School in Evesham.

Probably the first place that drew Ronald's attention was Sarehole Mill and millpond, as this was clearly visible back then from the front of 5 Gracewell

Cottages. There has been a mill on the site from at least the sixteenth century, but most of the three-storey brick mill buildings and chimney date from between 1760 to the 1850s.

The mill had two large water wheels and a steam engine, boiler and chimney to power the mill's machinery at times when water levels were too low to power the mill. Tolkien, and later his brother Hilary, would have peered through the dusty windows of the mill and marvelled at the mill machinery turning around and around as the corn was ground into flour.

The mill also ground peas and beans for animal feed and on other days would grind up bones for fertiliser for local farms. At the time you could sell the bones from your kitchen waste to the rag and bone man. Milling produced much dust and the miller would come out of the mill to chase off the Tolkien boys, for their own safety, covered in dust and surrounded by clouds of it. They nicknamed his son, George Andrew Junior, 'The White Ogre'.

Such a mill, with a smoking chimney, makes several appearances in *The Lord of the Rings*. When Sam Gamgee is looking into the Lady Galadriel's mirror he sees the mill of Hobbiton with a smoking chimney discharging pollution into the environment.

Sarehole Mill as Tolkien would have seen it, from the front garden of 5 Gracewell Cottages.

This vision seen by Sam is the mill as it is in *The Return of the King*, in the chapter 'Scouring of the Shire' when the Hobbits return to the Shire and find that the mill has become the mill in Sam's vision. So the mill we see today at Sarehole with its three-storey brick building and chimney is Ted Sandyman's mill in *The Lord of the Rings*.

The hero of **The Lord of the Rings***, Frodo Baggins, starts life in the book under the name of 'Bingo'. This name came from Tolkien's children's family of toy koala bears, which was known as 'the Bingos'. Frodo also started out as Bilbo Baggins' son, but later became his adopted heir following the death of Frodo's parents in a boating accident on the River Brandywine.*

After around four happy, almost carefree, years of living at 5 Gracewell Cottages, Tolkien finally passed his entrance examinations for King Edward's School on New Street in Birmingham city centre; this had also been his father Arthur's school. One of Tolkien's uncles paid the school fees, which were £12 a year, but Tolkien had to walk much of the 4 miles back and forth to school each day as the hamlet of Sarehole was well off the steam-tram lines.

Mabel decided to move to Moseley Village to get connected with the tram system, so they packed their belongings up and most likely loaded them onto a horse-drawn cart, or even a handcart, and travelled up Wake Green Road to Moseley Village.

The house they rented in Moseley Village was on the hill leading out of the village towards King's

Heath and was on the route of the steam trams ploughing back and forth, in and out of the city centre. The houses on the tram route were blighted because of the noise and smoke the trams produced and so the rents were lower. This was not a bad thing for Mabel, who by this time had been a widow for around four years and for whom money was tight with two young sons to bring up.

Tolkien did not like the house in Moseley, he thought it to be 'dreadful' and Moseley, with its noisy streets, smoky chimneys, horse-drawn traffic and lots of people, was such a change from the rural surroundings of Sarehole. Wherever he had moved to within the Victorian Birmingham suburbs, in the type of housing Mabel could afford, he would have had the same reaction.

Tolkien had always been a very plain dresser but by the 1960s he was wearing very colourful waistcoats. **The Lord of the Rings** *had made him a leading figure in the youth culture of the 1960s, even though at the time he was in his 60s and 70s.*

After a very short time in the house in Moseley the Tolkien family moved to King's Heath, to Westfield Road on the Grange Estate. This house backed onto the railway line and in those days coal was king and coal trucks from the South Wales coalfields were coming and going from King's Heath Station a short way from their house. The strange-sounding names on the trucks led to Tolkien discovering the Welsh language.

The Lord of the Rings *came out to mixed reviews in the 1950s: the American critic Edmund Wilson called the trilogy 'juvenile trash', while C.S. Lewis was criticised for his rave review of the books because of his friendship with Tolkien, and* **The Sunday Times'** *J. W. Lambert praised Tolkien for his extraordinary imagination.*

In 1902 the Tolkien family moved to Edgbaston, to 26 Oliver Road. The house was of poor quality compared to all the other houses they had lived in before, as all of these previous houses were only a few years old at the time they lived in them. The reason Mabel had moved to Edgbaston was so that they could attend the Birmingham Oratory Roman Catholic church. The family was soon befriended by the local parish priest, Father Francis Xavier Morgan, who was to remain a lifelong friend of Tolkien's and of his brother Hilary. Father Francis died in June 1935.

Tolkien was now, along with Hilary, attending St Philip's School, which was a short walk from their home in Oliver Road. The school was not to the same academic standard as King Edward's had been and Tolkien, who was not being academically challenged enough in his schoolwork, soon outpaced his classmates. Mabel took Tolkien out of St Philip's and after some tuition and cramming Tolkien won a Foundation Scholarship to King Edward's and returned there in the autumn of 1903.

In 1904 Ronald and Hilary contracted the childhood diseases measles and whooping cough, and because of the poor housing conditions at Oliver Road, Hilary also came down with pneumonia. The strain of nursing the two brothers took its toll on Mabel and in April 1904 she was taken ill and hospitalised and it was found that she was suffering from diabetes.

The house in Oliver Road was abandoned and the furniture was put into storage. Ronald was sent to stay with the family of his Aunt Jane's future husband, Edwin Neave, in Hove, and Hilary went to stay with his Suffield grandparents. Mabel came out of hospital in the summer of 1904 and went to convalesce in the village of Rednal, just outside Birmingham on the edge of the Lickey Hills.

The Hobbit *became a musical in 1967 when it was performed by the boys at New College School, Oxford. The story was adapted by Humphrey Carpenter and the music was written by Paul Drayton – Tolkien attended a performance.*

5

ANCIENT LANDSCAPES AND MYTHS

TOLKIEN'S FICTIONAL WORLD DREW on many of the ancient landscapes he visited during his life. Some had Anglo-Saxon legends and tales woven into them but dated back to earlier periods in history.

Some landscapes were very ancient indeed, such as the area around Lyme Regis where Tolkien and his brother would go on holiday with Father Francis after their mother's death. They would stop in the Three Cups Hotel, which was used as a film set in 1981 for the filming of *The French Lieutenant's Woman* staring Jeremy Irons and Meryl Streep.

Broad Street in Lyme Regis. The entrance to the Three Cups Hotel can be seen on the right-hand side of the picture.

The coastline around Lyme Regis is known as the Jurassic Coast as the beaches and cliffs are famous for their fossils – Tolkien once found a fossilised jawbone there that he thought must have come from an ancient dragon. His interest in dragons started in his childhood and his most famous fictional dragon is Smaug in *The Hobbit*.

After Tolkien's first year at Exeter College, Oxford, he went on a walking holiday in Berkshire, sketching the local villages and places he visited. In the 1930s Tolkien purchased his first motorcar, a Morris called *Old Jo* and shortly after that a newer model, called *Jo 2*. In these cars the family would go on trips to the Berkshire Downs in the area around the Uffington White Horse.

The white horse is believed to date from the Bronze Age and is 374ft long and 110ft wide and was constructed by digging trenches and then filling them with chalk rubble. It stands on the edge of the Berkshire Downs above a dry valley called the Manger, where legend has it that the horse goes to graze at night. It is best viewed from Dragon Hill, which stands below it, and also from the villages of

The Uffington White Horse viewed from above.

The smash hit of music hall in the early part of the twentieth century was J.M. Barrie's **Peter Pan,** *which Tolkien went to see in April 1910 at the Prince of Wales Theatre on Broad Street in Birmingham. Tolkien was very taken by the performance where Peter Pan, played by Pauline Chase, who was J.M. Barrie's goddaughter, actually appears to fly through the air, and wrote that this performance would stay with him for the rest of his life but regretted that Edith had not been with him at the theatre.*

Great Coxwell, Longcot and Fernham in the Vale of the White Horse.

In *The Lord of the Rings* the flag of Rohan is a running white horse on a green background, much like the Uffington White Horse. The rich fertile plain below the white horse, called the Vale of the White Horse, makes a very good model for the Plain of Rohan in *The Lord of the Rings*. Unlike the Plain of Rohan as depicted in the film version of *The Two Towers*, which was located on New Zealand's South Island, high in the Rough Ridge range with its rocky tors, boulders and outcrops.

Another monument that stands close to the white horse is Wayland's Smithy, a Neolithic chamber long barrow, renamed in the Saxon period after Wayland, the Saxon god of smiths and metalwork. Its Saxon connections would have most likely drawn Tolkien to visit it. Wayland flew to the Berkshire Downs from Sweden and made the tomb his home and forge after the King of Sweden stole a gold ring from his forge in Sweden. It is also said that no lesser a person than Merlin visited Wayland at the Smithy and, following this visit, Wayland forged Excalibur for King Arthur.

When the Hobbits are crossing the Barrow-downs in *The Lord of the Rings*, they become trapped in a barrow that sounds and feels like Wayland's Smithy. They are rescued by Tom Bombadil, a green man-like figure who was, strangely, based on Tolkien's son Michael's Dutch doll, who had a feather in his hat like Tom Bombadil did in *The Lord of the Rings.*

The Wayland's Smithy site was excavated in 1919 and again in the early 1960s, and has been dated to 3700, 3400 and 3350 BC. Today, it has been restored to its former glory and can be seen as a wedge-shaped long barrow. It is 180ft long, 48ft wide at the cross-shaped chamber end and 20ft wide at the tapered end, and the chamber end is guarded by huge sarsen stones.

In 1928 Tolkien was an advisor to the great archaeologist Sir Mortimer Wheeler at the excavations of the Roman temple site of Lydney, on the west bank of the River Severn in the county of Gloucestershire. The temple was in honour of the ancient British god Nodens, who was associated with healing, the sea, hunting and dogs. Tolkien wrote a report, 'The Name "Nodens"' following the excavation, which was reprinted in *Tolkien Studies: An Annual Scholarly Review*, volume 1V (West Virginia University Press, 2007).

During the excavation a lead curse tablet was found bearing an inscription cursing the person who had stolen a gold ring. A ring that matched the description of the ring on the lead tablet had been found by a farmer in the late eighteenth century, near to the Roman town of Silchester.

It is hard to determine whether Tolkien and Wheeler discussed this find, but they most likely would have. Could this ring and curse inscription be the spark in Tolkien's mind that led to the creation of the One Ring, or the 'precious' as Gollum called it, in *The Hobbit* and *The Lord of the Rings*?

Tolkien greatly admired the works of Arthur Rackham, especially his pictures and drawings of trees. Arthur Rackham illustrated many books, one of which was **Peter Pan in Kensington** *by J.M. Barrie, which contained fifty of Rackham's illustrations – the book became the basis of the stage play* **Peter Pan or The Boy Who Would Not Grow Up.**

In 1911, just before going to Exeter College, Oxford, Tolkien and his brother Hilary, along with his Aunt Jane and other family friends, made up a party and went on a climbing holiday in Switzerland. Here Tolkien was to first experience snowy mountains, crevasses and falling stones and boulders. These experiences would later emerge in his writings in books like **The Hobbit** *and* **The Lord of the Rings.**

The origins of Gandalf the Wizard can also be traced back to the holiday in Switzerland. Tolkien purchased some postcards as keepsakes of his holiday adventures in Switzerland, one of which was a reproduction of a painting showing a white-bearded old man wearing a cloak and a wide-brimmed hat sitting on a rock under a pine tree and talking to a white fawn. Many years later Tolkien wrote on the paper the postcard was stored in 'Origin of Gandalf'.

The ring, a chunky bezel mounted on a ten-sided hoop, has a primitive engraving of Venus on it and can be see at National Trust property the Vyne, in Hampshire. A copy of the ring along with the lead curse tablet can be seen at Lydney Park in Gloucestershire.

Close by is Lydney Camp, a British Iron Age promontory fort that was used during the Roman period to extract iron ore from the site, and the area is covered with open-cast workings or scowles and tunnels that still run through the hill. Local legend tells that these workings and tunnels were made by 'little people': hobgoblins and dwarves. During the early 1930s Tolkien started to write *The Hobbit* and there are many dwarves both in *The Hobbit* and *The Lord of the Rings*.

Tolkien's brother Hilary had a fruit farm at Blackminster in the Vale of Evesham; the two brothers were very close and the route that Tolkien would have taken from Oxford to Blackminster runs very close to The Rollright Stones. The stones have many Anglo-Saxon legends associated with them and Tolkien would most likely have visited the stones because of this.

The Rollright Stones are made up of a stone circle called the King's Men, which does look like jagged teeth sticking out of green gums (the grass), and a single standing stone called the King Stone, which looks like a landmark or a finger pointing upwards. The King Stone has suffered great damage over the years as people used to chip pieces off it: these pieces were believed to bring the owner good luck and keep the devil away! The nearby monument known as the Whispering Knights is a collapsed portal dolmen tomb.

The description of the standing stone and stone circle in the chapter 'Fog on the Barrow-Downs' in *The Lord of the Rings*, seems to fit Rollright quite well, especially on a foggy day in autumn:

> But even as he spoke he turned his glance eastwards, and he saw that on that side the hills were higher and looked down upon them; and all those hills were crowned with green mounds, and on some were standing stones, pointing upwards like jagged teeth out of green gums.
>
> (Tolkien, J.R.R., *The Fellowship of the Ring*, 'Fog on the Barrow-Downs')

A few lines further on:

> In the midst of it there stood a single stone, standing tall under the sun above, and at this hour

casting no shadow. It was shapeless and yet signifi-
cant: like a landmark, or a guarding finger, or more
like a warning.

> (Tolkien, J.R.R., *The Fellowship of the Ring*,
> 'Fog on the Barrow-Downs')

The Rollright Stones are sometimes called the
Stonehenge of Oxfordshire, even though the King
Stone is in Warwickshire as the county border runs
through the site.

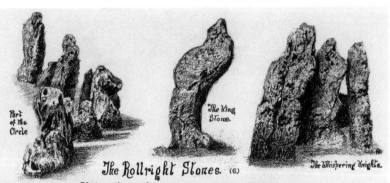

Part of the Circle

The King Stone.

The Whispering Knights.

The Rollright Stones. (6)

"The Stonehenge of Oxfordshire."

Situated on the last spur of the Cotswold Hills, about 3 miles from Chipping Norton. In the Circle are about 60 stones, the tallest of which is 7 feet 4 inches. On the other side of the road is the King Stone a monolith 8 feet high. East of the circle are the Whispering Knights, a Chromlech consisting of 5 large stones.

• 6 •

LOVE AND MARRIAGE

IN APRIL 1904 TOLKIEN'S mother Mabel was diagnosed with diabetes and in June 1904 she and her two sons Ronald and Hilary went to live in the village of Rednal on the edge of the Lickey Hills, just outside Birmingham. They had rooms in Hillside Cottage in the grounds of Oratory House, which had been built by Cardinal Newman as a retreat for the priests from the Oratory in Edgbaston. Hillside Cottage is now called Fern Cottage and can be rented as a holiday home.

Tolkien's mother Mabel died from diabetes on 14 November 1904; in her will she had appointed Father Francis Morgan, a Catholic priest from the Oratory church in Edgbaston, as guardian to the Tolkien brothers, Hilary and Ronald.

Duchess Road, Edgbaston around 1910. Cars would not have been a common sight at this time.

The brothers eventually went to live with their Aunt Beatrice Suffield in Stirling Road, Edgbaston, and in 1908 they moved to Mrs Faulkner's house: 37 Duchess Road, Edgbaston. As well as the Faulkner family there was a maid called Annie and a young female lodger called Edith Bratt, who had a bedroom on the first floor. The Tolkien brothers were in the bedroom above Edith on the second floor; Edith was a pretty 19-year-old with short dark hair and grey eyes.

Life at Exeter College could be a little on the wild side for young students like Tolkien. One evening, Tolkien heard raised voices in the distance; he ran out of college and joined a throng of fellow students who were 'ragging the town', a term used for mayhem and disorder by students. During this period of mayhem Tolkien and another student called Geoffrey hijacked a horse-drawn bus and drove it along Cornmarket to Carfax, by which time it had filled up with undergraduates. Here Tolkien left the bus and addressed the mob before moving on to the Martyr's Memorial outside Balliol College where he once more addressed the assembled crowd from the steps of the memorial. Tolkien was not disciplined for his actions that evening.

Edith was also an orphan like the Tolkien brothers: her mother Frances Bratt had died when she was 14 and after her mother's death she had gone to live at Dresden House School, a school for boarders in Evesham. The school was run by a pair of sisters known as the Misses Watts who had been taught music in the German city of Dresden, hence the name of the school. The school specialised in teaching music and this was where Edith developed her skill and love for playing the piano – even though she would have to rise at 6.00 a.m. and practise on the piano for around two hours before having breakfast.

Duchess Road was a jollier household than the Tolkien brothers' aunt's house in Stirling Road. Musical evenings were held and some of the Fathers from the Oratory attended these, at which Edith would play the piano. But, strangely, Mrs Faulkner would not allow Edith to practise her piano playing at any other time while she lived in Duchess Road.

After Tolkien's first term at Exeter College in 1911 he returned to Birmingham for Christmas and played Mrs Malaprop in Richard B. Sheridan's 1775 play **The Rivals** *at King Edward's School. Mrs Malaprop is a moralistic widow and the main comic figure in the play because she uses words that sound like other words but have a completely different meaning. Tolkien received good reviews for his portrayal.*

Edith and Tolkien, who was 16 at the time, became friendly and started walking out together, going into teashops in Birmingham, where the pair got up to mischief by dropping sugar cubes onto pedestrian's hats from first-floor balconies; ladies at this time did wear very large hats. The couple would have long conversations in the early morning or evening by leaning out of their bedroom windows and by the summer of 1909 they realised they were in love.

One day in late autumn 1909 the couple planned to go on a bicycle ride together; Edith set off first pretending that she was going to see her cousin Jennie Grove and Tolkien set off later, allegedly going to his school sports ground. The couple met up and cycled off to the Lickey Hills where they spent the afternoon, later calling at a house where Tolkien had spent some time studying for his Oxford scholarship. Here they were given tea to drink and then they cycled back to Duchess Road, arriving back at different times to make it look like they had been on different journeys.

The lady in the house where they had been given tea told Mrs Church, the wife of the caretaker at Oratory House, about Tolkien turning up with a young lady, and she in turn told the cook at the Oratory, Edgbaston who then told Father Francis. The couple's cover was blown!

Father Francis was very unhappy with Tolkien for what he considered to be having an affair with an older girl who lived in the same house as him. Father Francis was not only Tolkien's guardian but a father figure to him and his brother, and he controlled and gave money for their upbringing. Tolkien had to go and see Father Francis at the Oratory and was told not to see Edith again until he was 21. Father Francis told Tolkien that he wanted him to go to Oxford and not to waste his life on this young girl. Tolkien agreed to this as he had great respect and love for Father Francis, who also had control over his finances; he would require financial support if he was to study at Oxford.

The Hobbit *was published in the United States by Ballantine Books in August 1965 but failed to include Tolkien's revised text. The cover was a little strange as it had on it a lion, two emus and a tree with fruit on it. Tolkien was not very happy with this, thinking it was ugly, but thought that the publisher knew best on what sort of cover would sell the book in the United States. In February 1966 the book was reissued with Tolkien's revised text and the lion had gone from the cover.*

In 1956 **The Lord of the Rings** *was produced as a twelve-episode radio adaptation on the BBC Third Programme. Radio at the time was still the main home-entertainment medium and the Third Programme was the highbrow channel of the BBC network.*

While all this was unfolding, Tolkien went to Oxford to take his scholarship examinations, which he failed. Had he passed, however, he may have completed his studies at Oxford by the summer of 1914, and would most likely have joined the army like his brother Hilary did. Had he done so, he may not have survived the First World War.

In January 1910 Tolkien and his brother moved out of Duchess Road to Highfield Road, only a short distance away and just over the Hagley Road from the Oratory.

Tolkien and Edith had a further secret meeting when they took a train ride into the countryside, and they later bought each other presents for their birthdays, Edith buying Tolkien a fountain pen for his eighteenth birthday and Tolkien buying Edith a wristwatch for her twenty-first birthday. Both items would have been used daily by each of them and so acted as a reminder of the other.

Tolkien met Edith by accident outside the Prince of Wales Theatre on Broad Street in Birmingham. This was an answer to his prayers to meet her before she left to live in Cheltenham, where she was to live with Uncle and Auntie Jessop, who were old family friends. Tolkien and Edith also met several times in the street but at least one of these meetings was reported to Father Francis, who once again threatened to cut Tolkien off from financial support for his university education.

Edith left Birmingham on 2 March 1910 and Tolkien caught a glimpse of her cycling to the railway station – he thought that this was the last time he would see her until he was 21, and it was. Father Francis did let Tolkien write to Edith at Easter and she replied to him, saying that she was happy with her new life, which for a young woman of the time was quite an independent one.

All the time Tolkien was at Exeter College, Oxford he was only a short train journey of less than 50 miles on the GWR railway from Edith in Cheltenham.

> *In 1938 Tolkien was given a literary prize of £50 for the Best Children's Story of the Year for* **The Hobbit.** *This not-insignificant sum of money for the time was used to pay an outstanding doctor's bill, this being pre-National Health Service in Britain.*

Tolkien's next contact with Edith was just under three years later when, in the early hours of 3 January 1913, his twenty-first birthday, he wrote to Edith declaring his love for her and in so many words proposing to her. Edith replied that she was engaged to be married to an old school friend's brother, George Field, but did hint that she was doing this because she felt that she was 'on the shelf' – she was 24 years old at the time. She thought that Tolkien had forgotten her while he was at university but his writing to her changed matters. Tolkien arranged to visit Edith in Cheltenham on 8 January and after spending the day together Edith decided to marry Tolkien.

Edith left Cheltenham and moved to Warwick, where she and her cousin Jennie Grove took rooms and later a small house.

Edith started to take instruction in the Catholic faith at St Mary Immaculate Roman Catholic church under Father Murphy and she became a Roman Catholic on 8 January 1914. The date held great significance to the couple, being the first anniversary of their first meeting back in Cheltenham. During their time apart they had both become independent young adults and they had to rediscover one another.

On 3 July 1915 Tolkien was awarded a first-class honours degree from Oxford and on 9 July Tolkien's commission as a temporary second lieutenant was issued by the War Office. This was to take effect from 15 July, and he started his officer training in Bedford on 19 July. After Bedford, Tolkien trained in camps in Staffordshire but by early 1916 his training was coming to an end and he would soon be going overseas, so Tolkien and Edith decided to get married.

They married on Wednesday 22 March 1916 at St Mary Immaculate Roman Catholic church in Warwick, the ceremony performed by Father Murphy. The couple chose a Wednesday as it had been on Wednesday 8 January 1913 that their relationship had restarted in Cheltenham.

At Exeter College Tolkien became bored with his lectures in Latin and Greek but became very interested in his specialised subject, comparative philology, or the study of historical languages and comparing their relationship with other ancient languages. His lecturer for this subject was Joseph Wright. Wright, in all the sense of the words, was a self-made man who had started work in a woollen mill at the age of 6.

Wright taught himself to read and write at the age of 15 and then went to night school and studied French and German. By the time he was 18 he was running night-school classes from his bedroom for his workmates, charging them 2 pence a week, and once he had saved enough money he went to Germany to the University of Heidelberg. Here he studied old northern European languages, finally taking a doctorate in the subject. He then returned to England and eventually became professor of comparative philology at Oxford. Tolkien and Wright got on like a house on fire and Wright pushed Tolkien to drive his love of languages and education on to a higher level, which was just what he needed.

In the summer holidays of 1913 Tolkien took on the role of tutor and escort to two Mexican boys, accompanying them on a trip to France. They went to Paris where they were joined by another boy and their two aunts. Tolkien loved his visit to Paris but he had problems communicating with his party in Spanish and the locals in French. The party then went to Brittany to the seaside resort of Dinard and during their stay there one of the aunts was hit by a motor car on the pavement. She died a short time later and Tolkien had to arrange for her body to be returned to Mexico. Tolkien returned to England with the boys, vowing never to undertake a job like that ever again.

They honeymooned in Clevedon, north Somerset, for a week and Tolkien then returned to army life, going overseas on 4 June 1916.

After a period of fighting in the Battle of the Somme, Tolkien became ill with trench fever and returned to England and the First Southern Hospital, Birmingham University. He did not go overseas again as during the rest of the war he suffered repeatedly from trench fever and other illnesses, only having short periods of active army service.

While Tolkien was in the army Edith lived with her cousin Jennie and they relocated over twenty times to be close to Tolkien. Edith gave birth to their first son, John, in November 1917.

In the spring of 1914 Tolkien won the Exeter College Skeat Prize for English and was awarded £5.00 to buy books. He purchased a number of titles by William Morris who had been a student at Exeter College in the 1850s along with Edward Burne-Jones. The tapestry 'The Adoration of the Magi' designed by Burne-Jones and produced by Morris hangs in Exeter College Chapel.

After the war Tolkien, Edith, Jennie and John returned to Oxford and Tolkien's second son, Michael, was born in 1920. This was followed by five years at The University of Leeds where their third son, Christopher, was born and the family returned to Oxford in 1925. In 1929 their daughter, Priscilla, was born and for many years they lived happily in Oxford.

Edith died in November 1971 and Tolkien died in 1973. The couple are buried together in Wolvercote Cemetery in north Oxford.

7

CLUBS AND SOCIETIES

TOLKIEN WAS A MEMBER of many clubs and societies throughout his life. It all started at King Edward's School in New Street, Birmingham (he passed his entrance examination for the school in 1900). Tolkien's mother Mabel had sadly died of diabetes on 14 November 1904 and is buried in the Roman Catholic churchyard in Bromsgrove, Worcestershire. She had appointed Father Francis Morgan of the Oratory Church, Edgbaston to be the Tolkien brothers' guardian and they went to live with their Aunt Beatrice Suffield in Stirling Road, Edgbaston.

School must have been a 'rock' in Tolkien's life after the death of his mother. He had many friends within the school and it held many after-hours

A picture of Tolkien's House at King Edward's School from 1911. Tolkien can be seen on the front row of the picture second from the left next to Mr Measures, the housemaster. Tolkien's school friend and member of the TCBS (Tea Club and Barrovian Society) Christopher Wiseman can be seen on the picture on the front row, fifth from the left. (Picture courtesy of the King Edward's Foundation Archive)

activities for the boys, as it still does today. Tolkien was in Mr Measures' house, and eventually became house captain.

Tolkien played rugby football for his house but there was a price to pay for this. Tolkien was slight of build but by force of mind he drove himself on, taking some knocks and injuries on the way, one of which almost caused him to lose his tongue.

Tolkien also played rugby football for the school first team and eventually became the football secretary. He was a member of the school debating society and later its secretary and also a member of the school literary society, where he presented a paper on Norse sagas. He also performed in school plays. For a while he was a member of the King Edward's School Officer Training Corps and took part in a number of camps and exercises with the corps.

In 1911 Tolkien was a senior boy and had been appointed as a librarian in the school library along with some of his school friends: Christopher Wiseman, Robert Quilter Gilson, who was the headmaster's son, and a number of other senior boys.

In 1968 **The Hobbit** *was serialised on BBC radio in eight parts, produced by John Powell and staring Paul Daneman as Bilbo Baggins and Heron Carvic as Gandalf.*

These young men had time on their hands as most of the school in the summer term was taking school examinations. Tolkien had secured his place at Exeter College, Oxford, back in the December of 1910. They entertained themselves with jokes and fun but Birmingham, along with the rest of the country, was suffering a heatwave and maybe this drove them into making tea on a spirit stove fuelled by alcohol or methylated spirits. This is a dangerous practice in a library full of books and I wonder if Tolkien was reminded of this when he took the oath at the Bodleian Library in Oxford, part of which states the following:

not to bring into the Library, or kindle therein, any fire or flame, and not to smoke in the Library; and I promise to obey all rules of the Library.

Tolkien would have passed the Four Shire Stone, which stands on the Oxford Road just south of Moreton-in-Marsh, on his journeys from Oxford to the Vale of Evesham to visit his brother Hilary at his fruit farm. This could have been the model for the Three-Farthing Stone that marks the rough centre of Tolkien's Shire.

The Lord of the Rings *was made into an epic twenty-six-part series on BBC Radio 4; it was first broadcast on 8 March 1981 and ran until 30 August. It was produced by Jane Morgan and stared Ian Holm as Frodo Baggins; Ian was to play Bilbo Baggins in the three* **The Lord of the Rings** *films produced by Peter Jackson in the early 2000s. Gandalf was played by Michael Hordern the distinguished film actor and narrator of* **Paddington Bear.**

Members of the group, by this time known as the Tea Club, were taking it in turns to bring in nibbles and were also meeting out of school hours in Barrow's Store, just round the corner from the school in Corporation Street. This became known as the Barrovian Society, then later as the Tea Club and Barrovian Society and later the TCBS.

Tolkien went to Exeter College, Oxford, in the October of 1911 and the TCBS friends carried on meeting in various forms and at various locations into the First World War.

Geoffrey Bache Smith, a King Edward's boy some two years younger than Tolkien, joined the group after the death of Vincent Tought, another member. Smith was at Corpus Christi College, Oxford and, because of their school connections, became a friend of Tolkien's while Tolkien was at Exeter College.

Gilson and Smith both died in the Battle of the Somme in 1916. Smith had a work of poetry, *A Spring Harvest*, published posthumously in 1918 and Tolkien wrote the preface.

When Tolkien went to Exeter College, Oxford, he threw himself into college life; it is said that he joined all twenty-two college societies and even started his own, the Apolausticks (those devoted to self-indulgence). This was a lively group that held dinners, discussions and debates, and also had papers given – it was mainly made up of freshmen like Tolkien. This society was a bit like an Oxford college version of the TCBS of his school days and Tolkien did enjoy the company of his peers, where debate and talk flowed freely.

Tolkien was a member of the Stapeldon Society, so called because Exeter College had been founded by Walter de Stapeldon, Bishop of Exeter, in 1314, and for the first 100 years Exeter College was known as Stapeldon Hall. The Stapeldon Society was the college's version of a students' union and Tolkien started at the bottom of the society in 1912 as a member of the College Charges Investigation Committee. He became secretary in 1913 and the minutes written by him are still held at Exeter College. Tolkien became Stapeldon president in the spring term of 1914. He also played rugby for the college but did not row for them.

Tolkien served in the army between 1915 and 1918 during the First World War. He returned to Oxford in the October of 1918 and for a time worked on the *New English Dictionary* and later taught mainly female students from his home in Oxford.

He applied for the post of reader in English language at the University of Leeds in the summer of 1920. He was appointed to the post and moved to Leeds in the autumn of 1920.

At the University of Leeds he worked and collaborated with Eric Valentine Gordon, a Canadian who had been born on Valentine's Day in 1896 and had been a Rhodes Scholar at Oxford, where Tolkien had tutored him in 1920. They formed a club for under-graduates at the university called the Viking Club.

At Viking Club meetings Old Icelandic sagas would be read aloud and nursery rhymes were translated into Anglo-Saxon and read, along with songs and rude verses, often about students, mostly composed by Tolkien and Gordon. A collection of these songs and verses was privately published in a book entitled *Songs for Philologists* in 1936 but most copies were destroyed in a fire and it is said that around fourteen copies still exist; a copy was offered for sale some time ago for around $75,000. It is said that copious quantities of beer were drunk at the club meetings and the club made Tolkien and Gordon very popular with the students in the English department at the University of Leeds.

In 1953 Tolkien and Edith moved out of Oxford city centre to the North Oxford suburb of Headington to number 76 Sandfield Road. The house was a bit off the beaten track so Tolkien had to use taxis to get about in Oxford.

One event in the '60s that was to launch **The Lord of the Rings** *in a big way in the United States was the publishing of a paperback pirate copy of* **The Lord of the Rings** *by Ace Books. The problem was sorted out by the Science Fiction Writers of America, who got Ace Books to pay Tolkien royalties and stop publishing the book. The authorised version of* **The Lord of the Rings** *came out in America in October 1965 and with all the publicity over the pirate version the book became a huge bestseller.*

In 1925 Tolkien was elected Rawlinson and Bosworth Professor of Anglo-Saxon at Pembroke College, Oxford, and was part of the English faculty within Oxford teaching at a number of colleges. He met C.S. Lewis at an English faculty meeting in 1926 at Merton College and the two men become great friends. Lewis joined the literary group founded by Tolkien called Coalbiters (*kolbitar* in Icelandic meaning 'men who lounge so close to the fire in winter that they bite the coal') in 1927. The group met at Balliol College to read Icelandic sagas out loud to one another.

As well as the Eagle and Child, the Inklings also sometimes met in the Lamb & Flag; the two pubs face one another across the broad St Giles Street in Oxford. The Inklings as a group continued into late 1949, usually meeting on a Thursday evening in Lewis' rooms in the New Building, Magdalen College.

In the early 1930s the Coalbiters stopped meeting and a new literary group was formed by Edward Tangye Lean, an undergraduate from University College. This group was called the Inklings, and despite Lean leaving Oxford in 1933 and the group folding, the name did not die.

Tolkien and Lewis started having meetings with other like-minded academics in Lewis' rooms in the New Building, Magdalen College. They carried on calling this group the Inklings. It was made up of mostly Christian men and during the meetings readings and discussions of members' current and unfinished works would take place. This is where Tolkien first aired *The Lord of the Rings*.

Later, the Inklings met informally on Tuesday lunchtimes in the Eagle and Child public house, also known by the group as the Bird and Baby, or just the Bird. Meetings were held in the pub landlord's sitting room, known as the Rabbit Room, which is now incorporated into the pub and is like a shrine to the Inklings with pictures of Tolkien and other Inklings on the walls.

8

PLAQUES AND MEMORIALS

FOR A MAJOR TWENTIETH-CENTURY writer, Tolkien has very few plaques or memorials in England and these can be found in Birmingham, Oxford, Leeds, Bournemouth, Poole and Harrogate.

Birmingham has the most plaques but no statues, though in 2007 planning permission was granted for a 20ft-tall statue of an Ent (Treebeard) to be erected on the Green in Moseley Village, Birmingham. The sculptor commissioned to make this was none other than Tim Tolkien, the great-nephew of Tolkien and grandson of his brother Hilary. Tim's most famous work is 'Sentinel', a Spitfire sculpture in Castle Vale, Birmingham, but sadly the Ent sculpture has not yet been made.

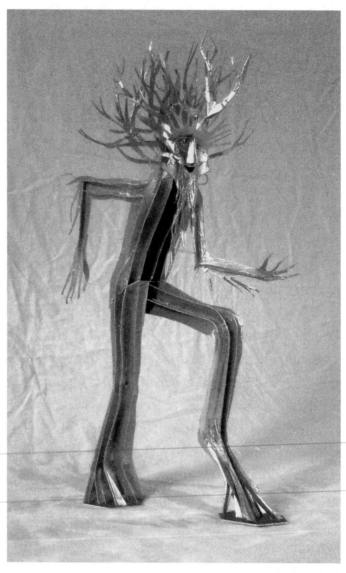

A model of the proposed Ent statue made by Tim Tolkien.
(Courtesy of Tim Tolkien and James Isgrove)

Sarehole Mill in Hall Green, Birmingham, boasts the newest blue plaque in Birmingham commemorating Tolkien's childhood in the area in 1896–1900; it was erected in 2002 on the wall of the miller's house. Tolkien had lived a short distance from the mill at 5 Gracewell Cottages and would have seen it every time he walked out of the front door of the house. The mill was to play a part in his fictional world of Middle-earth and a three-storey brick-built mill with a tall chimney, very similar to Sarehole Mill, appears in the chapter 'The Scouring of the Shire' in *The Return of the King*. Tolkien shares the plaque with the industrialist Matthew Boulton, two very strange bedfellows it must be said. The area around the mill hosts the Middle-earth Weekend each May to celebrate Tolkien's life and work.

In the September of 1914 Tolkien went to stay with his Aunt Jane at Phoenix Farm in Gedling, Nottinghamshire. His brother Hilary had also worked at the farm. While staying at the farm Tolkien wrote the poem 'The Voyage of Eärendel the Evening Star'; Eärendel would go on to be an important character in Tolkien's lifelong work The Silmarillion.

> *The chaperoning of ladies was a very important part of etiquette in the first half of the twentieth century. Father Francis once chaperoned Edith on a visit to see Tolkien in Oxford in his student days, for example. But after the First World War when Tolkien and Edith were living in Alfred Street, now Pusey Street, in Oxford, Tolkien could tutor young ladies from Lady Margaret Hall, at the time a ladies-only college, in Anglo-Saxon, because Edith would act as the chaperone for the students.*

A blue plaque recording Tolkien's life (1892–1973) and that he lived in the area from 1902–10 can be found on a modern building on the Hagley Road, close to the Five Ways road junction. A further blue plaque can be found on the last permanent address Tolkien had in Birmingham, on a children's nursery in Highfield Road, Edgbaston. Highfield Road is found opposite the Plough and Harrow Hotel on the Hagley Road, where another blue plaque can be found on the entrance to the hotel. This records that Tolkien stayed in the hotel in June 1916 and that the plaque was presented to the hotel by the Tolkien Society in June 1997; there is also a plaque in room 116, the room he stayed in with his new wife Edith before going to France and fighting on the Somme.

It is worth mentioning a blue plaque recording the life of the Birmingham surgeon J. Sampson Gamgee, who, among his many achievements, invented Gamgee tissues, cotton dressings for treating wounds, which are still used today. He died in 1880 but was still famous in Birmingham at the time Tolkien lived in Edgbaston, and Gamgee's widow lived just over the road from the house where Tolkien and his brother Hilary lived in Stirling Road after their mother Mabel's death in 1904. Sam Gamgee is the name of Frodo's Hobbit companion and manservant in *The Lord of the Rings,* and it is believed that Tolkien took the name from his boyhood memories of Birmingham. This blue plaque can be found on the side of the Repertory Theatre in Centenary Square off Broad Street in Birmingham city centre, which was the site of Gamgee's home back in the nineteenth century.

Oxford, Tolkien's home for most of his adult life and where he wrote *The Hobbit* and *The Lord of the Rings,* has a number of monuments to him. Tolkien attended Exeter College as a student between 1911–15 and after his death in 1973 his daughter-in-law Faith Tolkien sculpted a bronze head of Tolkien, which is on display just inside Exeter College chapel. The college is open to the public on a limited basis, so it may be worth checking the opening times if a visit is planned.

In 2003 on the island of Flores in Indonesia a number of hominid skeletons were discovered in a cave and were named **Homo Floresiensis** *(Flores Man) but they were nicknamed 'hobbit' because they only stood around 1m tall. They had lived into recent times, becoming extinct only 12,000 years ago. One of the scientific names proposed for them was* **Homo Hobbitus** *and they shared the island with Komodo Dragons!*

The only plaque recording Tolkien in the First World War can be found at 95 Valley Drive in Harrogate, where he was sent to recuperate in 1917 having contracted trench fever in France in 1916. The plaque reads:

 JRR Tolkien, author of 'The Hobbit', and 'The Lord of the Rings', stayed here in the spring of 1917, while recovering from the Trench Fever, he caught during the Great War, Harrogate Civic Society 2004.

Tolkien and his family lived in Leeds for around five years, first at 5 Holly Bank, rented from Cardinal Newman's niece Miss Moseley, then at 11 St Mark's Terrace, long-since demolished to make way for university expansion. In 1924 they then moved to the leafy suburb of West Park, living at 2 Darnley Road and it is here that the latest blue plaque to Tolkien can be found.

20 Northmoor Road, the blue plaque can be seen on the gable on the left hand side of the picture.

A close-up of the blue plaque.

> *Tolkien's three sons had their early education at the aptly named Dragon School, a short walk from their home in Northmoor Road, north Oxford.*

Tolkien purchased 22 Northmoor Road in north Oxford on his return to Oxford from Leeds in 1925, and in 1930 he purchased and moved into the house next door, 20 Northmoor Road. This had been the home of Basil Blackwell, the owner of Blackwell's bookshop on Broad Street, Oxford, before Tolkien moved in. A blue plaque is mounted on the front of the house recording that Tolkien lived there between 1930 and 1947.

The Eagle and Child public house on St Giles Street, Oxford was one of the meeting places in the 1930s of the literary group the Inklings, which included both Tolkien and C.S. Lewis as members. The Inklings called the pub the Bird and Baby and members would give readings from their current work. There is a small shrine to the Inklings and Tolkien inside the pub.

Tolkien lived at 3 Manor Road, Oxford from 1947–50 and 99 Holywell Street from 1950–53 but at the moment there are no blue plaques recording this. In 1953 he moved to 76 Sandfield Road, Headington and after Tolkien left in 1968 the new owner erected a stone plaque that stated 'J R R Tolkien lived here 1953–1968'. The plaque is over the garage, which Tolkien had converted into a study/library as he had not owned a car for many years.

Recent declassified documents from the Nobel Prize jury for literature have shown that C.S. Lewis nominated Tolkien's The Lord of the Rings *for a Nobel Prize in 1961. Anders Osterling, a judging jury member, wrote about* The Lord of the Rings: *'the result has not in any way measured up to storytelling of the highest quality'. Other authors nominated that year were Robert Frost, Graham Greene and E.M. Forster, with the winner being the Yugoslavian writer Ivo Andric.*

Tolkien and his wife Edith left Oxford in 1968 and moved to a bungalow at 19 Lakeside Road in Poole, Dorset. The bungalow has now been demolished but the two houses that replace it are called Lúthien and Beren, from Tolkien's 'The Tale of Beren and Lúthien', a love and adventure story of a mortal man, Beren, and an immortal Elf-maiden, Lúthien, first published in *The Silmarillion* after his death in 1973.

The reason that they moved to Poole was that Tolkien and Edith had often holidayed at the Hotel Miramar in Bournemouth and had enjoyed the mild climate, which helped to ease Edith's arthritis. The Hotel Miramar has a plaque recording that they had stayed there. The plaque reads:

John Ronald Reuel Tolkien, 1892-1973, Author and scholar, stayed here, regularly from, the 1950s, until 1972.

Tolkien's wife Edith died in November 1971 and Tolkien died in September 1973. The couple are buried together in Wolvercote Cemetery in north

Oxford. The grave is easy to find as it is signposted from the entrance of the cemetery. The inscription on the gravestone reads: Edith Mary Tolkien, Lúthien, 1889–1971, John Ronald Reuel Tolkien, Beren, 1892–1973.

After Tolkien's death he was remembered in his birthplace in 1984, when a memorial service was held at Bloemfontein Cathedral where he had been christened in 1892, and a plaque was erected at the site of his home, the Bank of Africa on Maitland Street, Bloemfontein.

A living memorial to Tolkien can be found in the University Parks, Oxford: two trees were planted in 1992 beside the River Cherwell to celebrate the centenary of Tolkien's birth. The trees are a silver maple and a golden false acacia, representing Telperion and Laurelin, the Two Trees of Valinor in *The Silmarillion*. Beside the path in front of the trees on the riverbank is a bench with a small plaque on it that reads as follows:

In Memory of J.R.R. Tolkien
1892–1973
This Bench and Two Trees Nearby
Representing Telperion and Laurelin
Were Donated by the
Tolkien Centenary Conference 1992

Lastly, a literally out-of-this-world memorial to Tolkien can be found in the main asteroid belt. In 1982 M. Watt discovered the asteroid, and in honour of Tolkien it is called 2675 Tolkien.

RELIGIOUS FAITH

TOLKIEN WAS A COMMITTED Christian for all his life. His mother and father, Mabel and Arthur, both came from Nonconformist families in Birmingham.

After her husband's death, religion in the form of high Church of England became a very important part of Mabel's life and each Sunday she and the two Tolkien brothers would walk to an Anglican church. At the time they were living at 5 Gracewell Cottages in the little hamlet of Sarehole on the southern edge of Birmingham and most places in Birmingham were a long hike away. One Sunday Tolkien found himself in a new church, St Anne's Roman Catholic church on Alcester Street in the crowed inner city suburb of Digbeth.

St Anne's church had been opened in 1884 but its roots lay in a church founded by Cardinal Newman in a disused gin factory before he moved to Edgbaston in 1852 and set up the Birmingham Oratory church.

In the spring of 1900 Mabel and her sister May Incledon (this was her married surname and she had also been in southern Africa when Mabel was living there), took instruction at St Anne's and entered the Church of Rome in June 1900.

In 1900 Mabel and the Tolkien brothers moved to Moseley Village and in 1901 the family moved to 86 Westfield Road on the Grange Estate in King's Heath. Here they attended the small St Dunstan's Roman Catholic church, which was made from iron sheet and clad inside with pine boards, opened in 1896. The church stood on the corner of Station Road and Westfield Road and was destroyed in the Second World War.

Mabel was looking for a more sympathetic church and once again they started going on long hikes to church on a Sunday and attending the

Oratory church in Edgbaston. In 1902 they moved to 26 Oliver Road, Edgbaston, a short walk from the church.

> *Tolkien was awarded his first-class honours degree on 3 July 1915 and this was announced in* **The Times** *newspaper on the same day; on 17 July* **The Times** *announced his commission as a temporary second lieutenant. So Tolkien's name had been mentioned in* **The Times** *twice in the month of July but for two very different reasons.*

The Tolkiens were soon befriended by Father Francis Xavier Morgan, the 43-year-old parish priest from the Oratory, who was to play a very important role in Tolkien's future life. Father Francis was very loud, humorous, sometimes embarrassing, kind and generous, and much loved by the Tolkien brothers; he became their guardian after Mabel's death in 1904.

Soon the Oratory became the orphaned Tolkien brothers' second home: they left their Stirling Road home early in the morning and then raced to the Oratory church to serve Mass for Father Francis at one of the side altars in the church. This was followed by breakfast in the Oratory refectory, then on weekdays off to school at King Edward's in Birmingham city centre.

When Tolkien went to Exeter College in Oxford in 1911 he attended St Aloysius Roman Catholic church on the Woodstock Road. The church was built in 1875 and at the time that Tolkien worshipped there, was served by the Jesuit Fathers. Cardinal Newman had preached there in the nineteenth century and had always dreamt of it becoming an oratory, and it became the Oxford Oratory in 1993.

In Tolkien's early student days he was a little wayward about attending Mass compared to his time at the Birmingham Oratory, but once he was reunited with Edith he mended his ways.

Fame for Tolkien had a dark side: his address and phone number at Sandfield Road were common knowledge and fans would call round to get books signed, give or send him sometimes strange gifts and invade the garden to take pictures through the windows of him and Edith. The telephone was also a problem, for fans, sometimes from as far away as the United States, would phone up with questions about **The Lord of the Rings** *or just to say hello. But, unaware of time differences, some of these calls would come in the middle of the night. To overcome this, Tolkien went ex-directory and eventually moved away from Oxford to Poole in Dorset.*

After Tolkien married Edith, she went to live in Great Haywood with her cousin Jennie because Tolkien, now in the army, was based at Brocton and Rugeley camps on Cannock Chase nearby. Because the couple had married during Lent they were unable to have the Nuptial Mass after the wedding ceremony. This was later carried out at St John the Baptist church in Great Haywood at Sunday Mass (see p.114). The church had been built in 1828 at Tixall Hall, about 3 miles away, as a private

chapel for the Aston family. It was moved to Great Haywood in 1845 and was part of the Archdiocese of Birmingham.

After the First World War, Tolkien returned to Oxford and in 1920 went to the University of Leeds as reader in English language, returning to Oxford in 1925 and buying a house in Northmoor Road off the Banbury Road, north Oxford. Tolkien was once again attending St Aloysius church (see opposite), sometimes cycling there to Mass at 7.30 a.m. with his sons and then returning home for breakfast.

Nave
Aloysius, Oxford

Tolkien also worshiped at St Gregory and St Augustine church on the Woodstock Road in Upper Wolvercote. In 1953 Tolkien and Edith moved to 76 Sandfield Road, Headington, north Oxford and here they worshiped at St Anthony's church on Headley Way. Four days after his death in September 1973, a Requiem Mass was held for Tolkien at this church and a memorial service was held on 17 November 1973 at Merton College chapel.

10

THE REAL MIDDLE-EARTH
(PLACES AND PEOPLE IN THE BOOKS)

TOLKIEN DREW INSPIRATION FOR some of the places and character names in his fictional world of Middle-earth from his life and the places where he lived and visited. Probably the first place in this list must be the little hamlet of Sarehole on the edge of Birmingham, where he lived from 1896–1900 aged 4 to 8. This was a very happy time for Tolkien and he did say in a 1966 interview in the *Oxford Mail*, quoted by John Ezard in the *Guardian* in 1991, that he based the Hobbits on the village people and children from Sarehole.

The place that dominated the view from the front of 5 Gracewell Cottages where he lived was Sarehole Mill and its millpond. In the foreword to *The Lord of the Rings* Tolkien does mention the miller

George Andrew and his son. He disliked the son greatly and called him the 'White Ogre', as he was often covered in flour dust, but he also says that the old miller was not named Sandyman, who was one of the millers in *The Lord of the Rings*.

A large brick-built mill with a tall chimney that sounds very much like Sarehole Mill appears in *The Lord of the Rings*, when Sam sees a vision of Hobbiton where the old mill has been pulled down and a large brick-built mill with chimney has replaced it. In the chapter in the third part of *The Lord of the Rings*, 'The Scouring of the Shire', when Sam and the other Hobbits return to the Shire, Sam's vision has come true and a large mill has replaced the old mill of Hobbiton.

A little way down the River Cole from Sarehole Mill is the ford of Green Lane, now Green Road. Because of the shape of the Cole Valley, the river is prone to flash flooding and this may very well have been the model for the ford at Bruinen. In the first book of *The Lord of the Rings*, this is the place where the Black Riders are washed away by a flash flood while pursuing Frodo, the Ring-bearer.

Across the fields behind Gracewell Cottages stood what Tolkien called 'a wonderful dell with flowers' (John Ezard, the *Guardian*, 1991); this today is called Moseley Bog and was once the main mill storage pool for Sarehole Mill, having been drained in the 1850s. The area that Tolkien would have known at the time he was living there would have been wet woodland, and during the summer months some of the woodland would have been dark and very atmospheric to the young Tolkien. This may well have been the inspiration for The Old Forest and Fangorn in *The Lord of the Rings*.

Moseley Bog may well have been the inspiration for Midgewater Marshes in *The Lord of the Rings*, which the Hobbits cross and in the process get bitten by midges, as today there are many small pools and springs where midges still breed and bite visitors in the summer and early autumn months.

In the interview in 1966 Tolkien talked about streams and another mill; this would have been Titterford Mill, which was pulled down in the 1920s. The millpool is still there today but now renamed Trittiford Mill Pool. This millpool, created in 1779, is very long and thin and may well be the model for Long Lake in *The Hobbit*.

Today all these places are in the Shire Country Park, which was set up in 2005 in honour of Tolkien's connections with the area.

On 1 December 1915 Tolkien had his first poem 'Goblin Feet' published in **Oxford Poetry** *by a national publisher, Sir Basil Blackwell, the son of the founder of Blackwell's bookshop in Broad Street, Oxford. At that time Sir Basil was the owner of the family publishing and bookshop empire. Many years later Tolkien and his family were to live at 20 Northmoor Road, which had once been Sir Basil's home, and this is where Tolkien wrote* **The Hobbit** *and most of* **The Lord of the Rings.**

In 1917 Tolkien was on active service in Yorkshire and Edith was living in furnished rooms in the village of Roos, near his camp. The couple would go on walks in the countryside when Tolkien was given leave, and on one such walk they came across a wood with an under-storey of hemlock. Edith sang and danced for Ronald on the woodland floor. Later, because of this event, Tolkien wrote 'The Tale of Beren and Lúthien', where Beren, a mortal man, falls in love with Lúthien, an immortal elven-maid. This became the central theme of **The Silmarillion.** *Tolkien considered himself to be Beren and Edith to be Lúthien, and the tale shows the love the couple had for one another.*

When Tolkien was living at Sarehole he would have walked back to his Suffield grandparents' house in Ashfield Road, King's Heath, and would have walked up Green Hill Road in Moseley – there is a place called Green Hill Country in *The Lord of the Rings*.

Tolkien's Suffield grandparents moved to Cotton Lane, Moseley, and Tolkien would visit them there; in memory of this he named one of the families in *The Lord of the Rings* Cotton: Farmer Cotton and his daughter Rose Cotton who married Sam Gamgee.

In 2006 **The Lord of the Rings** *became a stage musical, first in Toronto, Canada, and then a short-ened version moved onto the London stage in 2007 where it ran until 2008.*

When Tolkien moved to the Edgbaston/Ladywood border area, he was not living in the grand Victorian/Edwardian houses that Edgbaston is best known for but in the more working-class and middle-class housing in Oliver Road, Stirling Road and Duchess Road. This was a land of towers and chimneys, some on the skyline and others at the end of the road.

The towers and chimneys were to play a part in the development of his fictional world. At the end of Stirling Road stands the Edgbaston Waterworks with its wonderful Italianate-style chimney, partly designed by the famous architect John H. Chamberlain. A little further away stands the beautiful eighteenth-century brick-built tower known as Perrott's Folly, which stands 96ft tall, and inside there is a spiral staircase of 139 steps that links a small room on each floor. At the time when Tolkien lived in Stirling Road the tower was a weather station, so at night lights would go on and off on different floors as weather readings were being taken, giving the tower a sense of mystery.

The two towers in Edgbaston are locally believed to be Minas Morgul and Minus Tirith, two of the towers in *The Lord of the Rings*, the second book of which is entitled *The Two Towers*.

Another tower that Tolkien would have seen being built during his time living in Edgbaston was the University of Birmingham. This was the 315ft-tall Chamberlain Tower or 'Old Joe' as it is affectionately called after Joseph Chamberlain, the founder of the university.

At night the tower has four large illuminated clock faces, which can be seen from many parts of Birmingham and look like eyes looking at you, like the Eye of Sauron looking out from Mordor in *The Lord of the Rings*.

The University of Birmingham clock tower. (Courtesy of Kirsty Nicol)

After the First World War Tolkien returned to Oxford and worked part-time as an assistant lexicographer on the **Oxford English Dictionary** *at the Old Ashmolean Building on Broad Street, next door to Exeter College. Tolkien worked on the 'W' section of the dictionary; the work on the dictionary had been started by Sir James Murray in the 1880s, several years before Tolkien was even born.*

On the Hagley Road, a short distance from Stirling Road, stands the Victorian public house called the Ivy Bush, and the inn in Hobbiton on the Bywater Road is also called the Ivy Bush. It makes its first appearance on page two of *The Lord of the Rings*.

Tolkien's aunt, Jane, the sister of his mother Mabel, lived at Bag End Farm in the 1920s and early 1930s. The farm stands on the edge of the village of Dormston near Inkberrow in the county of Worcestershire. Tolkien visited the farm with his family during his Aunt Jane's ownership of it; much of the farm and surrounding buildings date from the sixteenth century.

When Tolkien was at the University of Leeds he worked with E. V. Gordon on **A Middle English Vocabulary,** *published in 1922, and fourteenth-century romance* **Sir Gawain and The Green Knight,** *published in 1925. Tolkien also marked examination papers for other universities during his summer holidays to supplement his income from the University of Leeds.*

Tolkien's heroes, Bilbo Baggins of *The Hobbit* and Frodo Baggins of *The Lord of the Rings* both lived at Bag End in the books, but their Bag End was a house made from underground tunnels. Tolkien himself did write that he had not made up the name Bag End but named it after his aunt's farm, which stood at the end of a country lane in Worcestershire. Today the farm is called Dormston Manor and is privately owned and strictly off-limits to visitors.

Oxford played a part in Tolkien's fictional world, and he did say that the Ratcliffe Camera looked like Sauron's temple to Morgoth on Númenor. He would have had a wonderful view of it from the

Fellows Garden at Exeter College when he was a student.

The college dining halls that Tolkien dined in as a student and later as a professor would also re-emerge in his later books. With the dais platform at one end of the hall for the college professors' high table and the students seated on forms (benches) and eating off long boards (trestle tables), they were reminiscent of Anglo-Saxon feasting halls, which were where this type of dining hall had its origins.

In 1972 Tolkien received two awards: a CBE from the queen at Buckingham Palace and an honorary Doctorate of Letters from the University of Oxford. This was not for his works of fiction but for his contribution to philology during his time at Oxford.

One of the leading characters in *The Lord of the Rings* is Sam Gamgee, who is Frodo's manservant, friend and companion, but the name has its origins in the famous Birmingham surgeon Dr Joseph

Sampson Gamgee. He was the inventor of Gamgee tissue, a cotton wool dressing for wounds, and although he died in 1886 he was still well known in Birmingham, and his widow lived over the road from Tolkien's lodgings in Stirling Road, Edgbaston.

In the 1940s Tolkien became a governor at King Edward's School in Edgbaston. His old school had moved out of the city centre in the 1930s, and one of the other governors was also a Gamgee, a descendent of Dr Gamgee: one Dr Leonard Parker Gamgee.

While on their honeymoon in Clevedon, north Somerset, in March 1916, Tolkien and his wife Edith went on a day-trip to see Cheddar Gorge and visit the caves. The caves were to re-emerge as the Glittering Caves in *The Lord of the Rings*. Tolkien revisited the caves just before writing this passage in the book in 1940 and was somewhat surprised to find how commercialised the caves had become since his first visit almost thirty years before.

Essex Bridge just outside the village of Great Haywood.

After Tolkien had returned from France in 1916 suffering from trench fever, he returned to Great Haywood in Staffordshire where he started to write *The Book of Lost Tales 1*. Three local places are believed to be the models for places in the book: Essex Bridge, Great Haywood and Shugborough Hall.

Essex Bridge is a fourteen-arched Tudor packhorse bridge across the River Trent, just above where the River Sow joins the River Trent. In *The Book of Lost Tales 1* Tolkien describes the village of Tavrobel standing by the confluence of two rivers with the Bridge of Tavrobel crossing the river. This could very well be Great Haywood and Essex Bridge.

On the other side of the River Trent from Great Haywood stands Shugborough Hall with its grand front-columned terrace, matching wings and eighty chimneys. In *The Tales of the Sun and the Moon* (*The Book of Lost Tales 1*) a gnome called Gilfanon owned a very old house, 'the House of a Hundred Chimneys', that stands by the bridge at Tavrobel. This does sound very like Shugborough Hall.

Shugborough Hall, Great Haywood.

11

THE GREAT CONFLICT: THE FIRST WORLD WAR

TOLKIEN DID NOT 'JOIN up' in the great patriotic call for men to join the army and navy in the late summer and early autumn of 1914 but returned to Oxford to complete his studies. However, he did join the Officers' Training Corps and drilled in the university parks several mornings each week, and also undertook training in map reading and signalling.

Tolkien's brother Hilary volunteered for military service in September 1914, joining the 3rd Birmingham Battalion as a drummer and bugler in the battalion band, but his main duties were that of a stretcher bearer. Edith Tolkien became his next-of-kin during the war and on several occasions received telegrams from the War Office to tell her that Hilary had been wounded.

In June 1915 Tolkien took his final examinations over a number of days at the Sheldonian Theatre on Broad Street and on 28 June 1915 he applied for a temporary commission in the army for the period of the war. He was awarded a first-class honours degree on 3 July 1915 and on 9 July Tolkien was commissioned as a temporary second lieutenant in the infantry; this was to take effect from 15 July.

In the 1950s there was a meeting of great minds from two sides of the literary world at the Eastgate Hotel. On one side were C.S. Lewis and Tolkien, and on the other were Arthur C. Clarke, science fiction writer, and Val Cleaver, a rocket scientist. Lewis and Clarke had corresponded for many years on the problems of mankind going to other planets because Lewis thought that mankind would take its evil ways with it. He based this view on human history. After a few pints and much conversation neither side had changed their views on the subject but they parted convivially, and Lewis' last words to Clarke and Cleaver were 'I'm sure you're very wicked people – but how dull it would be if everyone was good'.
(Arthur C. Clarke, Voices from the Sky*)*

On 19 July Tolkien went to Bedford to start his officer training in De Pary's Avenue where he learnt how to drill a platoon and attended lectures on military training.

As an officer Tolkien was required to grow a moustache, and he did. This rule became a problem, however, as German snipers would target soldiers with moustaches as a way of removing officers and so the rule tended to be relaxed.

By August Tolkien had completed his training and was posted to Whittington Heath Barracks in Staffordshire to join the 13th Battalion of the Lancashire Fusiliers, which had been raised in Hull in December 1914. This was a replenishment battalion, and the men were used to bring other units back to full strength after taking losses so Tolkien would not be going to the front with his sixty-man platoon.

In October, Tolkien and his battalion moved to the camp at Rugeley, still under construction, on Cannock Chase in Staffordshire and in December they moved across Cannock Chase to Brocton Camp. Both camps were made up of rows and

A view of Brocton Camp on Cannock Chase.

rows of low wooden huts but some troops slept in bell tents and each camp could hold around 40,000 men.

Training on Cannock Chase that autumn and winter was tough and bleak for Tolkien's platoon, who were learning the skills of modern trench warfare, digging zigzag trenches, bomb throwing, target practice, drilling, physical training, gas warfare and signalling.

Tolkien was to start training to become a signals officer. He had always been interested in languages during childhood, and codes are just another form of language. There was much equipment to learn about and master, and this included semaphore flags, heliograph used to flash Morse signals, lime-light lamps, dogs, carrier pigeons, despatch riders, runners, buzzers, rockets, telegraph and telephone systems.

On 6 June Tolkien embarked for France from Folkestone Harbour, docking at Le Havre, and he travelled to the massive army camps at Etaples, which the soldiers called 'eat apples', where he was billeted in camp 32.

Before leaving for France Tolkien and Edith devised a code of dots that Tolkien could insert into communications to her from France so that she could work out from these dots roughly where Tolkien was in France.

Storytelling started for Tolkien while he was at the University of Leeds. When his first son John was having problems going to sleep, Tolkien would sit on his bed and make up stories to help him fall asleep; sadly these tales were never written down.

All the time that Tolkien was in the camps the place was awash with rumours of the 'big push' that was to take place close to the town of Albert in the Somme region of northern France. On 27 June Tolkien finally got his orders to join the 11th Lancashire Fusiliers and travelled by train to the cathedral city of Amiens, which was full of troops from all over the British Empire. He joined his unit at Rubempre, some 14km north-east of Amiens, where they were billeted in the barns and outbuildings of the village.

On 1 July 1916 Tolkien was billeted at Warloy-Baillon behind the frontline and would have witnessed the final bombardment on the German front lines and the massive mines exploding under the German strong points just before 7.30 a.m. when the first wave of troops went over the top. The first day of the Battle of the Somme had been the greatest disaster in the history of the British Army with 19,240 dead, 35,493 wounded, 2,152 missing and 585 taken prisoner.

In mid-July Tolkien first saw action at the Somme in the attack on the village of Ovillers where, after two days of fierce fighting, the German troops in the village surrendered. On 21 July Tolkien was appointed battalion signal officer; he was now in charge of a large group of men who ranged from runners to telephone operators and in a mobile war they had to set up communications as and when the battalion moved around the battlefield.

In 1925 the Tolkien family were on holiday in Filey on the Yorkshire coast. By this time Tolkien's son Michael was almost 5 and carried a small lead figure of a dog everywhere he went. The figure of the dog was lost on the beach one day and Tolkien wrote the story **Roverandom** *as a way of explaining the dog's disappearance. The story was published in 1998, over seventy years after it was written.*

After this, Tolkien saw action in the trenches at Auchonvillers, Colincamps, Thiepval Wood (twice), the Leipzig Salient and Ovillers and helped capture Regina Trench on 21 and 22 October 1916. Tolkien and the fusiliers were taken out of the front line on Sunday 22 October. As they moved back, shells exploded around them and on their way to Ovillers they encountered a number of the new wonder weapons, with tanks grinding their way slowly up to the front line.

Tolkien had been at around fifty different locations since he arrived in France in June. Now relatively safe behind the front line, he was starting to feel unwell and on 27 October he reported sick to the medical officer with a high temperature. Tolkien was coming down with trench fever.

Trench fever was once described as 'a disease of squalor' and was caused by body lice, sometimes called chats (*pediculus corporis*). The lice infected the soldiers by feeding on their blood after the lice had become infected with trench fever by feeding on infected soldiers. The disease is caused by a bacterium called *bartonella quintana*, which lives in the stomach wall of the louse. Another route for infection was lousy troops scratching skin that had infected louse excreta on it: the excreta could remain infectious for several weeks.

At the time, the best treatment for trench fever was hospitalisation, so on 28 October Tolkien was admitted to an officers' hospital at Gezaincourt and the next day he was taken by ambulance train to Le Touquet on the French coast.

In 1920 Tolkien wrote his first Father Christmas letter to his son John, who was 3 years old, and for over twenty years he continued this spoof with his other three children, Michael, Christopher and Priscilla. At first the letters came from Father Christmas and the North Polar Bear but as time passed, more characters appeared, such as an elf called Ilbereth who was Father Christmas' secretary, and later elves and goblins also appeared.

The Father Christmas letters were beautifully illustrated by Tolkien and the envelopes sometimes had Polar postage stamps complete with dated franking on the envelope, and perhaps even a dusting of snow. The children would reply to the letters and leave their replies by the fireplace; these would disappear when no one was about. The last letter and pictures were sent in the dark days of the Second World War in 1943. Tolkien spent a lot of time creating this fictional world for his children. After his death the letters and drawings were edited by Baillie Tolkien, Christopher Tolkien's wife, and were published with the title **The Father Christmas Letters** *in 1976.*

In Le Touquet Tolkien was admitted to the Duchess of Westminster Hospital for Officers, which was in a converted casino on the seafront. The fever raged on for a further nine days and would not die down, so Tolkien was taken again by train to Le Havre and put onto the hospital ship HMHS *Asturias*, bound for Southampton, England.

HMHS *Asturias* would have offloaded her cargo of sick and wounded soldiers at Southampton docks, Tolkien would then have been put onto a hospital train bound for his old hometown of Birmingham. He would have arrived at Selly Oak railway station in Birmingham, most likely at night, and would have been transferred to a two-wheeled ambulance trailer towed by a civilian car.

So Tolkien was back home in Birmingham, the place of his boyhood and the early days of his romance with Edith. By early December, with good hospital nursing, his temperature had returned to normal but he was not yet 100 per cent fit, and still had many aches and pains. Tolkien went before a military medical board and was given six weeks to convalesce before returning to duty. He was to suffer further bouts of illness for the rest of the war, however, and never went overseas again.

Of Tolkien's peer group from school and college before the war, 243 former schoolboys from King Edward's School and 141 former students from Exeter College were dead. One of Tolkien's school friends and a member of the TCBS, Geoffrey Smith, who had dined with Tolkien during the Battle of the Somme, was killed in France on 3 December 1916. Tolkien mourned his death greatly and visited Smith's mother, now blind, in Birmingham in the 1930s; sadly, as well as Geoffrey, her other son was also killed in the war.

12

PRINCIPLE INHABITANTS OF MIDDLE-EARTH

WHEN TOLKIEN CREATED HIS fictional world of Middle-earth, he populated it with many different races and creatures, some drawn from mythology and others from his fertile imagination. Tolkien also had many different types of soldiers. Examples of these soldiers are the Riders of Rohan (cavalry soldiers), Orcs and Goblins (foot soldiers), Haradrim (dark-skinned soldiers from the Sunlands) and Easterlings (bearded axe soldiers).

Hobbits, not surprisingly, make their first appearance in *The Hobbit* and then in *The Lord of the Rings*, and are referred to in some of Tolkien's posthumously published works. The Hobbits of the Shire

A Hobbit on the road. (Courtesy of Ewa Kuczynski)

are short in stature, being between 2ft and 4ft tall with an average height of 3½ft; they are said to be a distant relative of the race of men. They are sometimes called 'little people' or 'halflings'.

Hobbits look well fed, with their rounded faces and stout build. They would eat six meals a day if they got the chance; they like simple, wholesome food that sounds like English food of the period that

Tolkien lived in. They usually have short, brown, curling hair and slightly pointed ears. Their most notable feature is their feet, which are covered in curly hair with thick leathery soles; because of this Hobbits very seldom need to wear shoes or boots. The hair on the feet is usually brown like the hair on their head.

A Hobbit man typically wears a brown or green jacket with gold or brass buttons, and under this is a red or yellow waistcoat. On their legs are breeches, sometimes made of green velvet, and for travelling or inclement weather a dark cloak with a hood is worn over their clothes.

While Tolkien was living at Northmoor Road he frequently cycled back and forth into Oxford for lectures and meetings on his high-seated bicycle. He was a common sight on the Banbury road as he would often return home for lunch, sometimes wearing his academic cap and gown. This meant that his children frequently had their father with them at lunchtime. He also regularly held tutorials for his students in his study at home.

To help with the housework at Northmoor Road the Tolkiens sometimes employed Icelandic au pairs, Tolkien had been taught to speak Icelandic by William Craigie some years before. Craigie had also helped Tolkien get work on the **New English Dictionary** *after the First World War.*

Hobbits live for around 100 to 130 years and do not come of age till they are 33 years old, and so only enter their middle age when over 50 years old. They can sit and talk about their ancestors for hours on end.

Hobbits live in 'Hobbit-holes', also known as 'Smials', which are usually found in hillsides, downs and banks and are entered through a round door that leads into a tunnel-shaped hall, usually panelled with wood and with tiles or carpet on the floor. The hall also has many pegs for visitors to hang their hats, coats and cloaks, as Hobbits love to have visitors to entertain and eat with. The tunnel-shaped passage leads out of the hall and off it can be found dining rooms, kitchens, bedrooms, large wardrobes, bathrooms and many pantries and cellars. All these rooms are on the same level so there are no stairs to climb in a Hobbit-hole and the accommodation is clean, dry and smoke free, except for the smoke from pipes. The best rooms are on the left-hand side of the hall as you enter through the round outer door and these rooms have round windows that look out onto the garden and the countryside beyond.

Hobbits like the simple life: good gardens and good farmland and only basic machines such as watermills, handlooms, blacksmiths' forges and hand tools. They are a peace-loving race and want to live a quiet, uneventful life, but when faced with peril and danger they are brave, courageous and resourceful. This can be seen during the War of the Ring, when Frodo Baggins and Samwise Gamgee go on the quest to destroy the Ring of Power. It can also be seen in the exploits of their Hobbit friends Peregrin (Pippin) Took and Meriadoc (Merry) Brandybuck, both on the quest to destroy the ring and later in their adventures during the War of the Ring. Tolkien may well have drawn the courage of these hobbits from his time on the Somme when he fought with a citizens' army made up of men who could not have dreamed of the horror, death and destruction they were faced with in the trenches of northern France.

When living at Northmoor Road in north Oxford,
Tolkien would sometimes dress up as a polar bear or
an Anglo-Saxon on New Year's Eve and would visit his
neighbours whilst wearing these disguises.

The early history of the Hobbits tells that there
were three different groups or clans of Hobbits living
in Middle-earth: the Harfoots, Stoors and Fallohides.

Living on the slopes of the Misty Mountains in
Hobbit-holes or Smials were the Harfoots, the largest
group of Hobbits in Middle-earth. They were very
similar in appearance to the Hobbits of the Shire.

The second-largest group of Hobbits were the
Stoors, who were shorter and stockier in build than
the Hobbits of the Shire and loved all things to do
with water, like boats and swimming. This is probably because they lived in the marshy area known as
Gladden Fields at the confluence of the two rivers:
the Anduin and the Gladden. The creature Sméagol,
or Gollum, came from this group of Hobbits but he
was much changed by the power of the One Ring
over the years that it was in his possession. The
Hobbits who live in Buckland and Marish in the
Shire may well be descendants of the Stoors.

The smallest group of Hobbits were the Fallohides, who liked to live in the woods below the Misty Mountains and were much more outgoing than other groups of Hobbits. They were said to be taller and fairer than the other two groups of Hobbits and were good leaders. Three of the leading Hobbits in *The Lord of the Rings*, Frodo, Merry and Pippin, were said to have Fallohides in their ancestry. Two Fallohide brothers, Marcho and Blanco, crossed the Brandywine River and founded the Shire on its west bank.

The Hobbit language at the time of the War of the Ring is called Hobbitish and is a local dialect of Westron, the native language of Men living in Gondor and Arnor. Westron is also known as the Common Speech and was the language used when different races of Middle-earth met and communicated, and was also used by the Dwarves and was the root of many Orkish languages.

Dwarves are larger than Hobbits but smaller than men; they are robustly built and have long, thick beards. Female Dwarves look very similar to their male counterparts but are outnumbered by three to one by the male Dwarves, and some of the peoples of Middle-earth do not believe they exist at all.

They are skilled fighters, hewing their foes with their axes. At the time of the War of the Ring there was great mistrust between Elves and Dwarves, but in *The Lord of the Rings* trilogy the Elf prince Legolas and the Dwarf Gimli become great friends and compete in friendly rivalry to see who has vanquished the most foes in battle.

Dwarves were skilled miners, digging deep into the earth to find precious stones and the metal mithril, which they prized above all other things. The Hobbits Bilbo and Frodo Baggins at different times in *The Hobbit* and *The Lord of the Rings* owned a mithril chainmail vest or corselet that was said to be worth more than the whole of the Shire. Dwarves were also skilled smiths and masons and liked to live in the mountains, caves and mines, like the lonely mountain Erebor, the Iron Hills, the Blue Mountains and the Mines of Moria or Khazad-dûm in the Misty Mountains.

The Race of Men, in Tolkien's mythical world of Middle-earth, was created by the One God Eru Ilúvatar, and he gave Men the 'Gift of Men', which was free will and mortality.

British and Indian cavalry attacking at the Battle of the Somme in 1916 – scenes like this may have been an inspiration to Tolkien's writing.

Tolkien had seen many troops from the British Empire and French colonies during his military service in France in 1916 and this could well have led to the many different races of Men that are found in Middle-earth during the Third Age. This is the period that *The Hobbit* and *The Lord of the Rings* are set in and the Third Age finishes at the end of the War of the Ring.

Tolkien sometimes purchased a barrel of beer, which he kept in the coal-hole at Northmoor Road, but Edith was not happy with this as she said it made the house smell like a brewery.

Rohirrim (horse-lord people) lived in Rohan, which they called the Riddermark, the Mark of the Riders or just the Mark. They lived in villages and farms on the lush grasslands of the Plain of Rohan, where they raised fine horses. The Rohirrim were tall with blond hair and fair faces, they lived for around eighty years and remained strong and fit into their old age. They were fine cavalry soldiers, known as the Riders of Rohan, but they also had fortresses such as Dunharrow and Helm's Deep. Helm's Deep was the name commonly used for the entire heavily fortified area of the Helm's Deep gorge, though the actual fortress there was called the Hornburg. The Rohirrim fought against Saruman in the War of the Ring, first being defeated at the two Battles of the Fords of Isen but winning victory at the Battle of the Hornburg with the help of Gandalf the Wizard and Huorns (trees).

Men of Gondor. Gondor was a Dúnedain kingdom located in south-western Middle-earth, bordered by Rohan to the north and Mordor to the east. It was founded by Elendil and his sons, Isildur and Anárion after the downfall of Númenor. The Dúnedain ('men of the west') were a race of Men descended from the Númenóreans that survived the sinking of their island kingdom. The Dúnedain were noble of spirit and body, but capable of evil if corrupted. They were often tall, with dark hair, pale skin and grey eyes. They were mighty warriors, skilled in the arts of battle.

Writing **The Lord of the Rings** *was usually carried out by Tolkien at night in his study. He first wrote in pen and ink on the back of students' old examination papers, replenishing his pen from time to time from an inkwell. Then, still using pen and ink, he copied the first draft out neatly and then he would type up chapters using a Hammond typewriter. Tolkien's daughter Priscilla also typed up some of the early chapters of* **The Lord of the Rings** *for Tolkien during the Second World War.*

Tolkien would hire a punt each year when his children were young and the family would go on punting expeditions up and down the River Cherwell, passing University Parks and beside the long thin manmade island called Mesopotamia. Mesopotamia is named from the Greek meaning 'between the rivers', referring to the area in modern-day Iraq between the Tigris and Euphrates Rivers. To reach the upper, quieter part of the River Cherwell, which Tolkien liked, they would take the punt up the roller ramp called Parson's Pleasure but the ladies in the punt may have had to avert their eyes as Oxford dons were allowed to sunbath in the nude on this section of the river in those days.

Gondor was considered to be the greatest kingdom of Men though its power waned over time and when the line of its kings failed it was ruled over by a line of stewards who swore to defend the kingdom and protect the throne until the rightful king appeared to claim it. After the defeat of Sauron, Gondor was ruled by Aragorn.

Men of Bree were a happy-go-lucky group of Men and got along well with the other peoples of Middle-earth; they were short in stature with brown hair. They were unusual in Middle-earth for being the only Men that lived alongside Hobbits, and at the Prancing Pony, the inn in Bree, there were even bedrooms designed for Hobbits with round windows to make them feel at home.

Orcs are the evil servants, or soldiers, of Sauron, best known in *The Lord of the Rings* as the Dark Lord of Mordor and Saruman the White, a Wizard in the service of the Dark Lord.

Orcs are usually squat, short, bow-legged and long-armed with dark faces, long fangs and squinty eyes, and they are usually soldiers skilled in the arts of tunnelling, manufacturing weapons and warfare. They are dirty and foul, and wear coarse woven clothes, heavy iron-shod boots, chainmail and iron helmets. They dislike beautiful things and go out of their way to destroy and kill them as well as eating the flesh of those they have killed, and it is said that they are also cannibals. Their medicines are usually nasty and fiery but work well to cure their illnesses and wounds.

While living in Oxford, the Tolkien family would holiday at the English seaside staying in resorts like Lyme Regis in Dorset, Milford-on-Sea, Lamorna Cove in Cornwall, Sidmouth in Devon and Weston-super-Mare.

The Orcs' weapon of choice is a scimitar-shaped sword but they were also skilled archers as well as being proficient in the use of spears, swords and knives.

Ents are around 14ft tall and look like a man that has become a tree, they are tree-herders, tree protectors and usually look after and care for the type of tree they look like. At sometime in Ent history the female Ents, called Entwives, who were wonderful gardeners and taught Man agriculture, became separated from the male Ents and are still lost.

Many Ents could walk and they had their own language called Entish, but they could also speak many of the languages used in Middle-earth. They were sustained by a nourishing drink called Ent-draughts. Compared to many other races of Middle-earth they were slow thinkers and slow to react to their thoughts but once roused they became like trees speeded-up, as they could destroy rocks and move large volumes of earth.

Ents were sometimes called 'Shepherds of the Trees' and the 'Shadow of the Wood' but the word *ent* comes from Old English meaning 'giant'. Treebeard, the oldest surviving Ent in Middle-earth, has a booming voice, which is said to have been based on the booming voice of C.S. Lewis.

> *Tolkien had a great sense of humour and one trick he liked to play was to hand shopkeepers his false teeth along with his money.*

Huorns were also Ents, or trees, that became dangerous and wild in the time of the Great Darkness, they were usually static but once roused could move very quickly. They were controlled by Ents and still had the power of speech, they were not evil but the one thing they hated was Orcs.

Trolls are evil creatures that live in Mordor and the Misty Mountains that are used as beasts of burden to carry heavy loads into battle and for pull-and-push engines of war. There are also fighting Trolls that are sometimes called Rock or Attack Trolls. They were created as a mockery of Ents and most Trolls dislike sunlight, some are even turned to stone if caught outside in the sunlight.

Wargs are large, wolf-like creatures, bred and corrupted by the Dark Powers, and are allies of Orcs and Goblins in Middle-earth.

Eagles are a race of noble large birds, Thorondor was the largest of their kind on Middle-earth having a wing-span of 180ft, and most Eagles were capable of flying while carrying a Wizard or Man, or a Hobbit and Dwarf. They are long-lived or could even be immortal; Thorondor's deeds were recorded over a period of just less than 600 years. Eagles rescued Gandalf from his imprisonment in the tower of Orthanc and rescued the Hobbits Frodo and Sam from the fiery slopes of Orodruin, also called Mount Doom.

Elves, sometimes called Folk of the Wood or Merry People, are the fairest race of Middle-earth, being around 6ft tall, of slender build and graceful in appearance, and were little effected by the variations in climate. They have keen senses and are able to see and hear much better than men and rest their minds by looking at beautiful things or in sleepless dreams instead of actually sleeping. They can communicate with one another through thought alone and love all things beautiful and the wonders of the natural world. They are wonderful archers, probably because of their heightened senses.

Elves were immortal so did not suffer the effects of aging or the ravages of diseases as did mankind, but they could be killed or die of grief, though it was only their bodies that died and not their minds. Elves were also great speakers and teachers as they taught the Ents to speak.

In the early 1930s, Tolkien took to the road in a Morris-Cowley called **Old Jo** and later a second Morris-Cowley called **Jo 2**; Tolkien was not a gifted driver and the book **Mister Bliss** may well in some parts reflect this. When going on holiday, the car would sometimes be loaded with the family luggage and Priscilla's soft toys and teddy bears while Edith, Christopher and Priscilla would travel by train. Tolkien's two older sons John and Michael would cycle down, a journey of two or three days, with stops to refresh themselves on West Country cider and with nights spent under the stars.

Wizards look like Men, usually appearing to be elderly, wearing long robes, tall hats and carrying a staff. Wizards are actually powerful beings sent to Middle-earth to guide and help the Free Peoples in the fight against Sauron. The colour of the robe indicates the Wizard's rank. Gandalf's robes are grey to start with but after his fight with the Balrog he reappears as a higher ranking White Wizard with white robes. A Wizard's power was channelled through his staff.

Dragons are evil creatures with huge, scale-covered bodies. They are very powerful and cunning and full of malice. They are also greedy and love to hoard treasure. To look into a dragon's eyes is dangerous as they can enchant their victims.

Father Francis Xavier Morgan, the Tolkien brothers' guardian after their mother died, was of Anglo-Spanish and Welsh descent, and his mother's side of the family were dealers in the sherry trade. When Father Francis died in June 1935 he left £1,000 to each of the Tolkien brothers in his will, a large sum of money at the time.

Black Riders are also known as Nazgûl, Ringwraiths and Fell Riders. They are nine powerful, evil, corrupted men who are the chief servants of Sauron and who are sent to find the One Ring. They ride black horses and winged Fell Beasts.

13

THE GREAT CONFLICT:
THE SECOND WORLD WAR

TOLKIEN WAS 47 YEARS old in January 1939 when he was contacted by the Foreign Office, who asked him if he was willing to work in their cryptographic department at a time of national emergency. He was happy to do this and on 27 March he went to the London headquarters of the Government Code and Cipher School (GCCS) for an instructional three-day course, which it is said Tolkien passed with flying colours. It is said that Tolkien was keen to become a codebreaker, most likely because of his life-long interest in languages and his special interest in Germanic and Old Norse languages.

Those who passed the course and agreed to sign up were offered an annual salary of £500, a large

sum of money at the time, but for some reason
Tolkien did not sign up.

GCCS moved out of London in August 1939 to
the now famous Bletchley Park to avoid the bomb-
ing that was expected if war with Germany started.

In October 1939 after the Second World War
had started, Tolkien was informed that his services
would no longer be required but many academics
did sign up and worked as codebreakers at Bletchley
Park and helped to shorten the war.

The outbreak of the Second World War was to cause
great changes in Tolkien's life: one of these changes
was that he became an air-raid precaution (ARP)
warden. His duties included patrolling local streets at
night during the blackout, checking that no light was
coming from houses. ARP wardens warned residents
displaying a light source by calling 'Put that light out'
or 'Cover that window'. Persistent offenders could
be reported to the police. Tolkien would have been
trained in fire fighting and first aid and during air raids
he would have patrolled the streets armed with sand-
bags to extinguish incendiary bombs.

Tolkien would have worn a uniform consisting of overalls and an armlet, a black steel helmet with the letter 'W' for warden painted onto it, a rattle to warn people of a forthcoming air raid and a gas-mask, though those were issued to everyone.

Luckily for Tolkien and Oxford, the city was not bombed because Hitler wanted Oxford to be his capital of Britain after the invasion that, thankfully, never came. So when Tolkien was on duty as a warden most of his time was spent sleeping in what served as the local headquarters: a damp hut.

In 1936 Tolkien gave his lecture 'Beowulf: The Monster and the Critics' in London at the British Academy and the lecture was published in the Proceedings of the British Academy that year. It was reprinted in 1983 in a collection of Tolkien's academic papers in The Monsters and the Critics and Other Essays, edited by his son Christopher Tolkien.

Two of Tolkien's sons joined the armed services: Michael became an anti-aircraft gunner and was awarded the George Medal for defending an airfield during the Battle of Britain. Christopher became a pilot and went to South Africa where he trained pilots and was kept updated by letters from his father on the progress of *The Lord of the Rings*.

Tolkien's oldest son John, who had been in Rome training to become a Catholic priest, returned to England and continued his training at Stonyhurst College, Hurst Green, in Ribble Valley in Lancashire. Tolkien visited him there and may have drawn some inspiration from the surrounding landscapes when writing *The Lord of the Rings*, but many parts of England may have influenced his writing as well.

On the domestic front, life was also changed: the aviary in the garden where Edith had kept budgerigars and other exotic birds in the warm summer days was converted into a henhouse where eggs and birds for the table were produced. Vegetables were growing on the site of an old tennis court and the home-grown produce helped when rationing was introduced.

Home life was also disrupted. Although Tolkien's three sons were away, his daughter Priscilla was still at home and sometimes lodgers and evacuees also stopped at Northmoor Road. In addition, there was little help for Edith around the house as domestic help was hard to come by during the war.

The war was to change university life, too: there were short courses for training officers and Tolkien generated a syllabus at the English school for naval cadets and made some of his lectures less specialised to cater to a wider audience.

During the war Tolkien met C.S. Lewis and Charles Williams at the White Horse public house on Broad Street, Oxford, where he would read some of his new writings from *The Lord of the Rings*. The White Horse is a very small public house so members of the public may well have had a preview of his forthcoming masterpiece. The pub may very well provide the name to a chapter in the book as the pub sign is that of a prancing pony and there is a chapter in *The Lord of the Rings* called 'At the Sign of the Prancing Pony'.

The sign outside the White Horse public house, Oxford.

Writing for Tolkien was a bit of a stop-start affair during the war, but one day in 1944 he went to Birmingham for an old boys' school reunion at King Edward's School. The school had stood in New Street, Birmingham, but had moved to a new site in Edgbaston in the 1930s. One of the reasons given for the move was a fear that the school could burn down as it backed onto the railway lines just outside New Street Station and sparks could come from the steam trains and start a fire in the school building. Strangely, a few months after the school moved to the new location the temporary school buildings on the new site did burn down!

Before going to his school reunion, Tolkien visited the old school site in New Street; he was not impressed by the 'modern' building, King Edward House, that had replaced his old school. But here he had a vision of ghosts rising from the pavement; this broke his writing block and on his return to Oxford he rapidly wrote the chapters 'The Passage of the Marches' and 'The Black Gate is Closed' in *The Two Towers*. These two chapters would draw on his First World War experiences in the trenches at the Battle of the Somme in 1916.

The war moved into 1945 and its final stages in Europe, and Tolkien was making little or no progress on *The Lord of the Rings*. Joy and tragedy came to Tolkien with VE Day on 9 May 1945 as it was the end of the conflict in Europe, but the next day Charles Williams was taken ill and after an operation he died on 15 May 1945.

Tolkien did not blame the Germans for the war, as he thought them to be a noble people, but put the blame on Adolf Hitler himself.

• 14 •

C.S. LEWIS

TOLKIEN FIRST MET C.S. Lewis in 1926 at Merton College at an English faculty meeting. Lewis was fascinated by Tolkien, who was talkative, but also a bit wary of him, because Tolkien was a Roman Catholic and a philologist and he had been warned against both these traits. Lewis had been born in Belfast in 1898 and was brought up as an Ulster Protestant. He was christened Clive Staples Lewis but at the age of 3 he decided that he wanted to be called Jack and was known as Jack by his family and friends all his life. He went to boarding school in the English town of Malvern and while at this school he lost his Christian faith.

Lewis had been at Oxford in 1916 but then joined the army and fought in the First World War as

Magdalen College New Building where C.S. Lewis had rooms.

an army officer. During active service in France he suffered from trench fever and was wounded during the Battle of Arras in April 1918 and returned to England. During Lewis' army service he became a great friend of Edward 'Paddy' Moore who was also Irish. The two men made a pact that if either was killed the other would support their family; Moore was confirmed dead in September 1918. Keeping his word, Lewis lived with Moore's mother until her death.

Lewis returned to Oxford in 1919 to study and after four years obtained three first-class degrees in

Greek and Latin literature, classic philosophy, and English language. His first permanent position was teaching English at Magdalen College. Lewis had rooms in New Building (built in 1733) at Magdalen College, where he lived during the week.

The Inklings sometimes met at the Lamb & Flag public house on St Giles, Oxford. The pub's name has religious connections, with the lamb representing a sacrificial lamb, symbolising Christ's death for humanity, while the flag is symbolic of Christ's victory over death in his resurrection.

Lewis and Tolkien rapidly became great friends, meeting in Lewis' rooms at Magdalen College and talking late into the night about their shared interest in Norse mythology. They often met on a Monday morning for a chat followed by a beer at the Eastgate Hotel, Oxford.

Tolkien helped Lewis return to a belief in God and Christianity in the late 1920s and early 1930s, and Lewis remained a committed Christian for the rest of his life.

After retiring from Merton College, Tolkien had to move all his books out of the college. He had a study-bedroom at Sandfield Road but by this time it was overflowing with his books, so Tolkien converted the garage into a study/library as he had not owned a motor car since the early 1940s. The moving of the books from college took several months and caused his lumbago to play up.

Once Tolkien had his study/library set up he began working on the book he had first begun in the First World War in 1916–17, **The Silmarillion,** *but this was not to be completed in his life time. It was published in 1977 having been edited by his son Christopher.*

Lewis' booming voice is believed to be where Tolkien got the idea for the booming voice of Treebeard, an Ent, in *The Lord of the Rings*. Ents are tree-like creatures that herd and protect the trees in the Forest of Fangorn and play a major role in the War of the Ring and the defeat of Sauron.

Tolkien and Lewis' friendship started to drift apart in the late 1930s, partly due to the arrival of Charles Williams from London. Williams worked for the Oxford University Press, which moved to Oxford in 1939, and Lewis was coming under the influence of Charles Williams, who, among many things, was a writer of spiritual thrillers.

Lewis died in the November of 1963 and Tolkien wrote of Jack Lewis to his son Michael a few days later:

We were separated first by the sudden apparition of Charles Williams, and then by his marriage. Of which he never told me; I learned of it long after the event. But we owed each a great debt to the other, and that tie with the deep affection that it begot, remains. He was a great man of whom the

cold-blood official obituaries only scraped the sur-
face, in places with injustice

(Carpenter, H. and Tolkien, C.,

The Letters of J.R.R. Tolkien)

The two men were literary giants of the twentieth
century, with Tolkien best known for *The Hobbit* and
The Lord of the Rings and Lewis best known for *The
Chronicles of Narnia*. Many of these books have now
been made into films in the late twentieth and early
twenty-first century.

15

OXFORD COLLEGES

TOLKIEN'S FIRST EXPERIENCE OF Oxford colleges was in early December 1909 when he stayed at Corpus Christi College on Merton Street to take his university scholarship examination. He failed to gain a scholarship award and returned to Birmingham in low spirits. He returned to Oxford in December 1910 having prepared hard for his examination and this time he passed: on 17 December he heard that he had been awarded an Open Classical Exhibition, worth £60 a year, to Exeter College, Oxford.

At the end of the second week of October 1911 Tolkien and another former student of King Edward's School, L.K. Sands, were taken to Oxford by motorcar by R.W. 'Dickie' Reynolds, who had taught English literature at King Edward's School.

At Exeter College Tolkien had a bedroom and sitting room in the college building known as Swiss Cottage that fronted onto Broad Street, but Tolkien's rooms looked out onto Turl Street.

Tolkien's name was painted on a board at the entrance to the building and there was a 'scout' – a college servant – who would bring Tolkien breakfast, and lunch, which usually comprised beer, bread and cheese. In the evening there would be dinner, a formal event in the college dining hall (see below).

In 1913 Tolkien sent a picture postcard of the dining hall at Exeter College to Edith Bratt marking where he sat with a cross, the location was in the middle of the hall opposite the fireplaces. Not a bad spot in the winter.

Tolkien played rugby for the college but did not take up rowing. The all-male college lifestyle suited him, as he was happy in the company of like-minded students.

In the Junior Common Room 'Suggestions Book', Tolkien wrote that the college needed to purchase a good English dictionary; most of the other students' comments were usually about college food!

Tolkien was reading Classics but soon became bored with Greek and Latin: his main interest was Germanic literature. In 1913 he took his Honour Moderation examinations but failed to achieve a first. The head of Exeter College, Dr Farnell, knew that Tolkien was interested in Germanic languages and Old English and arranged for Tolkien to study at the English School in 1913, where he specialised in Old Norse.

Tolkien took his final examinations for the Honours School of English Language and Literature at the Sheldonian Theatre on Broad Street in June 1915 and achieved first-class honours.

After service in the British Army during the First World War, followed by a short period back in Oxford and then working for five years in the English department at the University of Leeds, Tolkien returned to Oxford in 1925.

Tolkien had been elected Rawlinson and Bosworth professor of Anglo-Saxon by the casting vote of Joseph Wells, the vice-chancellor of Oxford University. The appointment was to Pembroke College, which is located around Pembroke Square and Beef Lane off St Aldates, opposite Christ

Church College. The appointment to Pembroke College was to give Tolkien college support and the social side of college life, but he was to teach on a faculty basis, and taught students from many Oxford colleges.

Tolkien sometimes lectured at Pembroke College and at the Examination Schools on the High Street, giving very popular lectures on subjects like the epic Anglo-Saxon poem *Beowulf* and the Middle English poem *Sir Gawain and the Green Knight*. He was a quietly spoken lecturer, possibly due to the rugby accident he had at school when he almost bit off his tongue. It is said that he made his lectures come to life, and, in the case of *Beowulf*, took his students back to the mead halls and feasting of the poem.

Tolkien was contracted to give at least 36 lectures a year but usually did 72–136 in order to fully cover the topics of Anglo-Saxon and Middle English, and he also held tutorials for his students. He remained at Pembroke College until 1945 and it was during this period that Tolkien wrote *The Hobbit* and most of *The Lord of the Rings*.

Another thing that Tolkien had to deal with from Sandfield Road was an ever-increasing volume of fan mail, which he had diligently dealt with by himself — but as the flow turned into a torrent he needed help. To this end, he employed a number of part-time secretaries who with the passage of time became great friends with Tolkien and Edith.

In 1945 Tolkien was elected Merton College professor of English language and literature, becoming a professorial fellow of Merton College. The college fronts onto Merton Street and the back of the college looks out onto Merton Fields over a section of the old town wall, and beyond this is Christ Church Meadow with the River Thames or Isis flowing at the bottom of the meadow. He had rooms in the Fellows' Quadrangle, overlooking the meadows.

Tolkien liked Merton College; it was more relaxed and less formal than Pembroke College had been and he wrote to his son Christopher Tolkien in October 1945:

Merton College from the Fields, Oxford.

It is incredible belonging to a real college (and a
very large and wealthy one)

(Letter 103 in Carpenter, H. and Tolkien, C.,
The Letters of J.R.R. Tolkien)

Tolkien was to give new lectures in the history of
English language and English literature to the period
of Chaucer, as well as having to undertake his work
at Pembroke College until a new Rawlinson and
Bosworth professor of Anglo-Saxon was elected.

During his time at Merton College the three
books that make up *The Lord of the Rings* were published: *The Fellowship of the Ring* in 1954, *The Two
Towers* in 1954 and *The Return of the King* in 1955.

Tolkien retired from Merton College in 1959 but his relationship with the college did not end there. In 1966, when he and Edith had been married for fifty years, they celebrated their anniversary at Merton College.

After Edith's death in 1971 the college came to Tolkien's rescue and he became a resident honorary fellow of the college. He lived in a flat in one of the college houses, 21 Merton Street, and so in a strange way he had gone full circle, as his first experience of Oxford had been at Corpus Christi College in Merton Street in 1909.

One of the highlights of the Oxford year is the Eights Week boat races held at the end of May on the River Thames or Isis. Tolkien was a great fan of the races, going to watch them from college-barges moored on the banks of the Thames. Strangely, most Hobbits were uncomfortable with boats and rivers and most could not swim.

16

PUBLISHED WORKS
OF J.R.R. TOLKIEN

This is a chronological list of Tolkien's published works to date. There are many different editions and reissues of most of the titles.

A Middle English Vocabulary (Oxford: The Clarendon Press, 1922).

Tolkien, J.R.R. and Gordon, E.V. (eds), *Sir Gawain & The Green Knight* (Oxford: The Clarendon Press, 1925).

The Hobbit: or There and Back Again (London: George Allen and Unwin, 1937).

Farmer Giles of Ham (London: George Allen and Unwin, 1949).

The Fellowship of the Ring: being the first part of The Lord of the Rings (London: George Allen and Unwin, 1954).

The Two Towers: being the second part of The Lord of the Rings (London: George Allen and Unwin, 1954).

The Return of the King: being the third part of The Lord of the Rings (London: George Allen and Unwin, 1955).

The Adventures of Tom Bombadil and Other Verses from the Red Book (London: George Allen and Unwin, 1962).

Tree and Leaf (London: George Allen and Unwin, 1964).

The Tolkien Reader (New York: Ballantine, 1966) (contains 'The Homecoming of Beorhtnoth Beorthelm's Son', 'Tree and Leaf', 'Farmer Giles of Ham' and 'The Adventures of Tom Bombadil'.)

Smith of Wootton Major (London: George Allen and Unwin, 1967).

The Road Goes Ever On: A Song Cycle (Boston: Houghton Mifflin, 1967; London: George Allen and Unwin, 1968).

WORKS PUBLISHED POSTHUMOUSLY

The Father Christmas Letters, edited by B. Tolkien (London: George Allen and Unwin, 1976).

The Silmarillion, edited by C. Tolkien (London: George Allen and Unwin, 1977).

Pictures by J.R.R. Tolkien, edited by C. Tolkien (London: George Allen and Unwin, 1979).

Unfinished Tales of Númenor and Middle-earth, edited by C. Tolkien (London: George Allen and Unwin, 1980).

Letters of J.R.R. Tolkien, edited by C. Tolkien and H. Carpenter (London: George Allen and Unwin, 1981).

Mr Bliss (London: George Allen & Unwin, 1982).

The Monsters and the Critics and Other Essays, edited by C. Tolkien (London: George Allen and Unwin, 1983).

The History of Middle-earth series, twelve books in total, edited by C. Tolkien (London: George Allen and Unwin; Unwin Hyman; HarperCollins, 1983–96).

Roverandom, edited by C. Tolkien (London: HarperCollins, 1998).

Unfinished Tales, edited by C. Tolkien (London: HarperCollins, 1998).

The Children of Húrin, edited by C. Tolkien (London: HarperCollins, 2007).

The Legend of Sigurd and Gudrún (London: HarperCollins, 2009).

• BIBLIOGRAPHY •

Blackham, Robert S., *The Roots of Tolkien's Middle-earth* (Tempus, 2006)

———, *Tolkien and the Peril of War* (The History Press, 2011)

———, *Tolkien's Oxford* (The History Press, 2008)

Carpenter, Humphrey (ed.) with the assistance of Tolkien, Christopher, *The Letters of J.R.R. Tolkien* (Unwin Paperbacks, 1990)

Carpenter, Humphrey, *J.R.R. Tolkien: A Biography* (Unwin Paperbacks, 1978)

———, *The Inklings* (Harper Collins Publishers, 2006)

Clarke, Arthur C., *Voices From The Sky* (Mayflower Paperback, 1969)

Exeter College Oxford (Exeter College, Oxford)

Foster, Robert, *The Complete Guide to Middle-Earth* (Unwin Paperbacks, 1978)

Gardner, Angela and Murray, Jef, *Black & White Ogre Country* (ADC Publications Ltd, 2009)

Garth, John, *Tolkien and the Great War* (Harper Collins Publishers, 2004)

Morton, Andrew H. and Hayes, John, *Tolkien's Gedling* (Brewin Books, 2008)

Morton, Andrew H., *Tolkien's Bag End* (Brewin Books, 2009)

Scull, Christina and Hammond, Wayne G., *The J.R.R.Tolkien Companion and Guide* (Harper Collins Publishers, 2006)

Shippey, Tom, *The Road to Middle-Earth* (Grafton, 1992)

Tolkien, J.R.R., *Farmer Giles of Ham* (Harper Collins Publishers, 1993)

———, *Mr. Bliss* (George Allen & Unwin, 1982)

———, *Roverandom* (Harper Collins Publishers, 1998)

———, *Smith of Wootton Major* (Unwin Hyman Ltd, 1990)

———, *The Hobbit* (Unwin Books, 1967)

———, *The Lord of the Rings* (George Allen & Unwin Ltd, 1968)

Tolkien, John & Priscilla, *The Tolkien Family Album* (Harper Collins Publishers, 1992)

Wilson, A.N., *C.S. Lewis: A Biography* (Harper Collins, 1991)

Wright, Joseph, *An Elementary Middle English Grammar* (Oxford University Press, 1928)

Also available in this series:

978 0 7509 9228 2

The History Press

The destination for history
www.thehistorypress.co.uk